RAVING FA

Brilliant, educational…one of the best how-to books I have read. Every author would benefit from having this in their writer's toolbox. Not only does she illustrate how to, but she does an excellent job of spelling out the pitfalls and things many authors do that perhaps "shouldn't" be done. From character development to plot, Ms. Jump explores every aspect of writing a story from beginning to end. It's an entire weekend conference in one book.

—Catherine Bybee, New York Times bestselling author

"Jam-packed with tools, tricks, and field-tested strategies, Shirley's Jump's direct, delightful book lives in the nitty-gritty between expedience and experience. It's a charming, chatty writing guide that rewards rumination and revisits to help anyone craft compelling fiction."

—Damon Suede, award-winning author

"Clear and insightful, *Writing Compelling Fiction* is a gem of a book for both the novice and the veteran writer. Shirley's experience as a teacher and presenter shines through…it's an invaluable resource."

—Donna Alward, *New York Times* bestselling author

"No one knows the craft of writing better than Shirley Jump. Whether you're writing your first novel or are an experienced author, *Writing Compelling Fiction* is a must-have addition to your writing library."

—Barbara Wallace, Amazon bestselling author.

"A great guide to writing fiction, whether you're a beginner or a published author. Shirley's practical lessons break complex ideas into actionable steps, and the homework at the end of each chapter show you how to apply them to *your* work. Highly recommend."

—Laura Drake, award-winning author

WRITING COMPELLING FICTION

Master the Fundamentals of Unforgettable Stories

NEW YORK TIMES BESTSELLING AUTHOR

SHIRLEY JUMP

Writing Compelling Fiction
Master the Fundamentals of Unforgettable Stories
By Shirley Jump
Part of The Authority Series

TABLE OF CONTENTS

INTRODUCTION

It doesn't take a rocket scientist to figure out that you probably picked up this book because you want to be a better writer. Heck, I wrote this book to help you be a better writer and answer all the questions that people ask when I teach online or speak at a conference. And, to be honest, I wrote it to remind myself of what goes into writing a truly compelling book, because the truth is, there's a lot to remember when it comes to getting from *once upon a time* to *the end*.

But if you want to write a book that matters, a book that makes a difference, a book that you are so stinking proud of writing that you practically bust a gut talking about it, then this is the one you want to read, because I'm going to tell you exactly how to do that. This book is the compilation of decades of hard-knocks learning, great editors, and studying my craft. I put it all in one place so that you don't have to be a slow learner like I was.

I've always been a writer, and frankly, have no other life skills (so if you bought this book, thank you for funding the only career I am capable of having). However, the road to becoming a fiction writer was long and bumpy, and nearly didn't happen for me.

I started out as a journalist when I was eleven (by lying about my age and getting a job at a newspaper). I moved on to copywriting, magazine articles, and public relations. Deep down inside, however, I always wanted to write novels. I took a class in writing a romance novel at my local community education center and figured I knew everything I needed to know. After all, I had a degree in English and years of experience writing. Transitioning to fiction should be a piece of cake, right?

Wrong. It was incredibly difficult.

But I was doggedly determined, or maybe too dumb to know when to stop trying. I kept writing, kept submitting, crying over rejection letters, and most of all, believing. When I was trying to get published back in the days of cavemen and the invention of fire, there was no such thing as self-publishing. The only route to becoming a fiction author was selling to one of the New York publishing houses.

I wrote ten books in eight years, and every last one of them was rejected by editors in New York and England (because why stop at one country for rejections when you can have two?). I thought I had a sale on the table in the spring of 2001, but at the last second, it fell through. Then I had a book that had already been rejected by Harlequin that then went on to win my local writer's group contest, and as a first-place winner, I got a request for the full manuscript by a senior editor in a different department at Harlequin.

At Harlequin, resubmitting a book they've already said no to is the kiss of death. They keep notes on what they've already seen, and they know if you try to circumvent the system, so I had to be honest if I sent it back to Harlequin. My agent at the time refused to represent the book because she thought it would make her look bad, so I sent it in myself in May of 2001.

Then I got another rejection letter for a different book, and my then-agent told me that I clearly didn't have what it took to write fiction, and maybe I should just quit. I was devastated.

If my own agent didn't believe I could do it, and clearly none of the publishers I'd sent my books to thought I was good enough to be published, then surely I wasn't. At that time, I had my second non-fiction book coming out (which went on to hit *The Wall Street Journal* bestseller list) and I had more than two thousand articles published in national publications, but none of it mattered anymore. My dream, ever since I was old enough to read, had been to write fiction.

My spouse at the time was not the most supportive person. I had to fight for my time to write, getting up at 4:30 a.m. for years, fitting my fiction around kid duty and working full-time. He didn't see the point in me going to writer's group meetings, because I clearly wasn't going to sell anything. I was making really good money copywriting for ad agencies, but hated that work so much, I could sympathize with a wolf who chews off his own leg to escape a trap.

When my agent rejected me, it was the last straw. The only person who was saying "you can do this" had finally said "no, you can't. You suck." Okay, those weren't her exact words, but the meaning was the same. In desperation, I called Harlequin to check on the status of my submission, hoping they'd say they were too busy drawing up my contract to get back to me.

Instead, they said they had lost my manuscript in the myriad of submissions they received. I took it all as a sign that my agent was right, and I wasn't meant to write fiction.

That day, June 23, 2001, I threw everything out. Took the how-to books off the shelves, tossed the manuscripts, wiped the hard drive clean and threw out the disks. I packaged my entire writing life into three Hefty garbage bags, then sat down in my office and had myself a damned fine pity party.

I had finally given up on myself and my dream.

On that day, my then-husband encouraged me to put everything back, told me I'd someday sell a novel, and tried to get me to write again. But I wouldn't. In fact, I couldn't. The spark had disappeared for me and I figured I was fighting a losing battle anyway. I spent a good week feeling really miserable. I binge watched reality TV and didn't write a single word.

Then, the following Saturday, a package arrived in the mail. A big package. Priority mail. Clearly, it was the manuscript I'd sent to Harlequin. Since the whole thing had been returned to me, I chalked it up as a rejection and tossed it in the trash unread. My theory (based on hundreds of rejections) was that they always send you a letter to reject you; they call if they want to buy.

But I couldn't *not know,* so I fished the package out of the trash and started to read the enclosed letter from the senior editor of Harlequin Romance. "Dear Shirley," it began, "I love this book and would be interested in buying it if you revised..."

I was astounded. The door I had thought was forever closed to me had suddenly opened an inch. Two weeks later, I'd signed with a new agent. Three months later, I sent the revised book in and...just before Christmas of 2001, my new agent called with the news I'd waited all my life to hear.

My book had sold.

The end result of that story, *The Virgin's Proposal* (now reissued as *Kissing Mr. Wrong*), was in bookstores in January 2003 and went on to win the Booksellers' Best Award for the Best Traditional Romance of that year, which seemed like poetic justice. As of today, I've published more than eighty books in twenty-four countries, hit all the major bestseller lists, and won multiple awards for my work.

And yet, I'm continually astounded when I see one of my books. It's still a pinch-myself moment to see a cover with my name on it. And I feel a constant drive to be a better author today than I was yesterday.

That's why I'm writing this book. Not just to give you information and tons of writing exercises that will help you improve as an author, but to give you some encouragement and faith. Publishing can be a vicious, soul-sucking industry, but it can also be one of the most rewarding things you accomplish in life. When I get a letter from a reader saying my words helped her forget the chemo she was undergoing, or that my character reminded her of her late grandmother, it makes my day. I know my book has touched someone, and that's worth more than reviews and royalties.

Writing a fabulous book, however, is about more than just the thousands of words that go between the first page and the last page. Those words shouldn't be just any words, they should be ones that are compelling. Words that impact the reader. Words that they remember and treasure and tell their friends they must read.

That's what *Writing Compelling Fiction* is here to teach you, and what I hope you take away from every page of this book. Your words matter—to you, to your reader—and you'd better damned well make sure they are the most powerful words you can create. That's your duty as an author, a keeper of stories, and a narrator who helps the rest of us get through life.

PART ONE
COMPELLING PLOTS

CHAPTER ONE
BUILD A BETTER FRAMEWORK

Have you ever watched a house being built? The construction crew pours the concrete foundation, and then they start on the framing. They don't start with installing those cute Shaker-style kitchen cabinets or that really cool marble pedestal sink. What people see and experience when they walk into the house is the Setting, which gives them an emotional and visceral reaction, but that's not where it all starts. And neither should your book.

Think about it. You could write the prettiest prose this side of the Mississippi and craft metaphors that would make Herman Melville drool, but none of those elegant words are going to grab a reader if the foundation isn't there. It's all a bunch of pretty details sitting in a jumble on the floor. Sort of like our imaginary house. That amazing pedestal sink with the brass handle and copper bowl has no floor or walls to be mounted on, and the cabinets are just stacked on the ground.

The foundation and framing are the most important parts of the house, and the one area where you don't want to skimp on cost. Because, you know, it's kinda dangerous if the house falls down on your head.

In a book, the Plot is the foundation and framing. It's where you need to spend a nice chunk of time in the planning stages, and not go for the easy, quick, trite solution. The Plot is built on a concept called Goal, Motivation, and Conflict, three things that make your story hang together and move forward.

The Basics of GMC

You probably already know that in every book, there are two types of Goal, Motivation, and Conflict for every major Character: External and Internal. All major Characters (heroes, heroines, protagonists, antagonists) will have both an Internal and External GMC.

The Goal is what the Character wants.

The Motivation is why they want it.

The Conflict is the buts (roadblocks)
that keep getting in the way.

External GMC is tangible—a job, money, a move, etc. Something that has external (outside of the Character's emotions) impact. The External Goal should be something vitally important to the Character, *something that he or she will fight to achieve.* A Goal is a journey, essentially, and we want that journey to be worth the hours we invest in that Character. Make the External Goal tough, maybe even impossible, to achieve, and make it one that matters deeply to the Character and to the Character's life.

The Internal GMC is emotional. Your Character may or may not even be aware of what he wants emotionally (e.g., acceptance, forgiveness, inner peace). That's okay, as long as you, as the author, know. We'll get into more on how you create the External and Internal Goals in a sec. Just hang with me while I explain how it all works.

Romance is NEVER the Goal

A side note for romance writers: A common mistake that writers make in romance novels is Setting an External Goal of finding love. While most of us want to be loved and to find someone to love, that is rarely, if ever, our primary Goal in life. We want that raise to pay for our child's surgery. We want to sell the house so we can move closer to a dying relative. We want to get revenge on the man who killed a loved one. Just as people do in real life, your Characters should have External and Internal Goals that are outside of the romance.

But I'm writing a romance, you say. That's a major part of the Plot. Yes—sort of. It's a major complication in the Plot. Love comes along at the worst possible time for your Characters. Let me say that again, because it's important to remember:

> In a love story, love comes along at the
> worst possible time for the protagonists.

Why? Because falling in love forces them to make choices and decisions that impact the External and Internal GMC. What does that create? Conflict. And what does lots of Conflict create? An engaging, powerful, compelling book that readers can't put down. Oooh, sounds like a recipe to follow, doesn't it?

Take Kennedy Ryan's RITA® winner *Long Shot,* for example. In that book, her hero and heroine meet when the heroine is already dating someone else, and the hero is on his way to the NBA. The reader can see that there is a love potential there, and the Characters can see it, too, but pursuing that romance would mean changing their current life courses. Both think they are on the right path at the time they meet, so they say goodbye (and our hearts break!). When the Characters meet again and again, that budding love is still there, but for various complicated and conflicted reasons (jobs, children, etc.), they don't get together. That continual Tension kept me turning the pages to see if they could make it work and made me sad when their External and Internal GMCs kept them apart. August and Iris are continually separated by the lives they have chosen. Why? Because falling in love only complicates things for them.

In addition, neither is ready for their love story internally. They both have some growing and changing to do to be deserving of their happily ever after. Watching that growth is also part of the page-turning quality of this book and was beautifully done. August and Iris aren't handed their ending on a silver platter— they work for it and richly deserve it, because they solve their inner emotional problems. Ask any therapist—if you want to have a healthy, long-term relationship with a partner, you have to get your emotional ducks in a row first. Otherwise, all your baggage is going to get in the way. It works the same for your Characters.

Let's play devil's advocate here and say Author Annie does make falling in love the Goal. Her heroine, Romantic Ronnie, wants to find her prince and fall in love. She isn't working toward anything else in the book—getting ahead in school, earning a promotion at work, repairing her family relationships, finding a house—nope, she's focused solely on finding true love.

If you were Romantic Ronnie's best friend, wouldn't you say to her, "Get a life, Ronnie! There's more to your world than love. You need to build a strong, independent life for yourself before you bring anyone else into it." Any therapist (or good friend) will tell you that a person whose entire world revolves around their love interest (can anyone say codependency?) ends up putting the relationship ahead of their own self-needs. If that relationship ends, Romantic Ronnie's world is completely devastated because her world orbited around Prince Playboy. And no one wants to read about that because frankly, that kind of thing just makes people angry, because we all know Romantic Ronnie is just going to skip her weekly CODA meeting and lose herself in the next relationship she has.

By creating Characters who have External and Internal GMCs that are *not* about finding love, you create Characters the reader can respect and root for. You create Tension on every page. You create a love story that requires sacrifice and choices. In short, a rich, deep book that readers love.

Work Backwards to Build Out

After over eighty published books, I've got a pretty strong opinion on what makes for a compelling story. I think creating a great Character, along with a strong Plot, creates a

Character-driven book, which is more emotional (and thus more memorable and compelling). It also means that every move your Character makes and every choice he makes should be true to his Character.

When you start a new book idea, you very likely have a vague idea of your Character. Even if it's something as simple as *Charlie Character is an accountant in Iowa who just got divorced.* Here's the question I want you to ask yourself as you're developing Charlie:

What is your Character's Worst Nightmare?

We will be getting into the Worst Nightmare in depth in the section on Compelling Characters, but here I want to talk about how it ties into your Conflict and Plot. Your Character's Worst Nightmare is the thing they least want to do. It stems from deep emotional issues and fears. Like the germophobe who is forced to dive into a germ-infested sewer. Or the control freak who has to hand over the reins to someone else. That Worst Nightmare feeds into their Deepest Emotional Fear (ah, there you are, Internal GMC!).

Their Worst Nightmare should morph into the *What If*—which is the Story Question, and the basis of GMC. What if a germophobe had to step out of her comfort zone and spend weeks in a Third World country with minimal health care and sanitation? What on earth would drive a germophobe to go to a place devoid of Purell and Lysol on purpose? That *Why* is the Motivation.

Maybe you're thinking there's no way a germophobe would go to a Third World country and eventually dive into a sewer. But…would she do it if her child was trapped? Would she do it if she were escaping a killer? Most likely, yes, because those are some pretty powerful Motivations for her actions.

By knowing your Character's Worst Nightmare, you create a Goal that she needs to achieve so badly, she'll face her Deepest fears, both *Externally and Internally*. Rising stakes are a natural by-product of a Plot that stems from the Character's Worst Nightmare, and Rising Stakes create…compelling novels.

Now, I know I've thrown a lot at you already in the first few pages of this book, but don't worry. We're going to dissect all of it in depth over the next pages. I'm here to walk you through it all, one piece at a time.

Deciding on Goals

As I said before, the Goal, in short, is what your Character wants. Whatever you choose as the Goal, make sure it's big enough to carry the entire story. Does your Protagonist want to launch a new business? Find his birth mother? Rescue his child? Those are big, important Goals that the reader will root for. They also take time to achieve, which means they can last over 30,000 to 100,000 words. If the Goal is too small, the reader won't care, and you won't have enough framing to build from, like trying to build a five-bedroom house from a pallet of plywood. Something like "find a good pen" isn't enough of a Goal. However, you can take a seemingly small, unimportant Goal and make it big by adding powerful Motivation.

Take *Shrek*, for instance. All he wants at the beginning of the movie is to get his swamp and privacy back. Not a big Goal—on the surface. Shrek desperately wants his swamp back because his Worst Nightmare is being with people and being rejected (his Deepest Emotional Fear). In order to get his swamp back, he has to face, and eventually conquer, both his Worst Nightmare and Deepest Emotional Fears. If you haven't watched the movie, do it today. It's a fantastic example of Worst Nightmare and Deepest Emotional Fear at play.

A book-length External Goal should also have multiple steps that feed into it in order to achieve it. Rescuing a child, escaping a killer, saving the family home, etc., are all the kind of goals that have many steps involved. Those steps become your Scenes. For instance, if Jane Doe's book-length goal is to start a new career in L.A., she must search for a job, pack her apartment, find a new place to rent, embark on a road trip, etc. That's a pretty boring goal, unless you add a whole lot of conflicts and maybe a murderer on her tail, but you get the idea. Whatever your character needs, there should be many steps to achieve it. No one wants to read a novel about a Goal that is achieved in five pages.

Shrek's goal to get his swamp back entails a lot of big steps for a reclusive ogre (which means each of the scenes also challenges his Internal Goal, Motivation, and Conflict, and forces him to grow and change). Going to Duloc, confronting Lord

Farquaad, rescuing the princess, interacting with Donkey, etc. He has a quest and a journey to undertake, and every single step is out of his comfort zone.

> **The best External Goals force the Character to confront his Deepest Emotional Fears at every turn.**

Characters who are comfortable, who have it easy all the time, are simply not interesting. The reader is going to stop caring, and stop being riveted by the story, if everything the Character does works out well and with minimal effort. Sort of like when you have a friend who says "oh, I'm going on a diet" and she loses five pounds a week by just cutting out dessert. You start to hate her and get to the point where you don't want to hear one more word about her easy weight loss. Characters who struggle, who overcome impossible odds, and who fight for an important Goal are compelling, interesting, and memorable.

Choosing Motivations

Motivation is key. Your reader will go along with pretty much anything if the Character is properly motivated. You can have a mother kill her own child and with the right Motivation, make the reader weep for the mother. Think of *Sophie's Choice* by William Styron—the mother is force by the Nazis to choose one of her two children to save. The one she gives up is going to the gas chamber. She knows she is sentencing one of her children to death. It's a horrific choice, but oh, the Motivation.

Remember, there are no hard and fast rules when it comes to writing. We all have different creative processes. This book is my advice and my thoughts, and if you write a different way, I'm not going to come over to your house and take your keyboard away. I promise. Make this information work for you, however that takes shape.

Not every Plot has to have such heart-wrenching Motivations. However, they should be strong and ideally, there should be more than one Motivation for the external Goal (we'll get to Internal Goals in a second). Charlie Character can be desperate for a raise at the beginning of the book. But if his only Motivation for that raise is to buy a cherry-red Maserati and pick up hot girls, your reader will hate his vapid shallow self. Instead, if his Motivation for the raise is to pay for a life-saving surgery for his child or to have enough money to move his family to a safe neighborhood (or both!) then you have strong Motivations. Look at TV shows (like *Good Girls*, for example) where Characters have deep Motivations to do things that we would otherwise hate them for. *Good Girls* is built on the premise of three ordinary moms who become career criminals. Their Motivations and Conflicts are what make that TV show successful and relatable.

Relatability is important. If your reader can understand and relate to your Character's *Why* (their Motivation), they will go along on that journey right to the end. If they can't, they will put the book down and move on to another.

Create More Conflict

So many writers go too easy on their Characters. Remember what I said about respect and relatability? We want to be impressed by how hard the Character works and what they will sacrifice along the way to achieve their Goals. Your book should be filled with Conflicts, which are all the roadblocks that get in the way (for Shrek, it's the castle, the dragon, Donkey, the princess herself, the interlopers/friends he doesn't want, and many more). Why? Because Conflict creates Tension, Tension raises stakes, and raised stakes keeps readers reading.

The Internal is Just as Vital

The Internal GMC is a little trickier because chances are your Character is completely unaware of what they want emotionally (or they are only glossing over the surface). People don't tend to stand around and think, *Gee, I really would love to be accepted for who I am.* Or *Wow, it sure would be nice to forgive myself for that accident.* Neither do Characters (see relatability above). The Character who says he wants closure really—deep down inside—wants to find out who he is and why he was abandoned by his mother.

Shrek, for instance, wants privacy. But deep down inside, he really wants to be loved for who he is (Internal Goal) because no one has ever seen past his ogreness (Internal Motivation).

But in his heart, he's afraid he will never fit in and never be enough, and is terrified of rejection (Internal Conflicts). He risks all of that by standing up in a public venue in front of the very people who hunted him down for being an ogre. He does it because he has finally learned (growth!) that if he doesn't, he will never have what he truly wants deep, deep down inside in his little green ogre heart—to be loved and respected exactly as he is, by others and more importantly, by *himself*.

> I recommend figuring out your GMC and then putting that into sentences that you keep nearby while you write. That helps you keep the Plot on track and not wander off the path.
>
> **External GMC:** Character wants *what* (External Goal) *because* (External Motivation) *but* (External Conflict) gets in the way.
>
> **Internal GMC:** Character wants *what* (emotionally; Internal Goal) *because* (emotional Motivation) *but* (emotional Conflict) gets in the way.

A Few Tips

Increasing the stakes and making things worse until your Characters finally learn the lessons they need to in order to deserve their HEA (Happy Ever After) or HFN (Happy For Now) are the keys that keep the reader turning the pages. Read Debra Dixon's book, *Goal, Motivation and Conflict* for more explanation and some great correlations to movies to help you understand this concept.

Once you figure this out, you're ready to start writing. When you get stuck in the Plot, go back to this chart and evaluate. As we get deeper into this book, we will talk about applying this on a Scene-by-Scene basis to make your Scene and Sequel come alive. If you're getting bogged down in your book, go back to those two sentences I recommended you write and ask yourself if you have gone off track and added a wing to the house without a blueprint (your friendly neighborhood building inspector and your contractor will tell you that's never a good idea). Whatever doesn't feed into those statements has to go.

Your Turn:

We're going to delve into Motivation in the next chapter, so your assignment is easy (or seems easy on the surface): Goals. For each of your main Characters (Protagonists and/or Antagonists), I want you to write out their External and Internal Goals. Remember, the External Goal should be something tangible that takes a while to achieve and is worth the reader investing time in reading about it, and the Internal Goal should be driven by emotional needs.

My Character Wants: External

                         Internal

Scene Analysis

Read the following snippet of the opening scene from Midnight Kiss, New Year Wish, and see if you can pinpoint Jenna's External and Internal Goals.

Thick, wet, heavy snow tumbled onto Jenna Pearson's shoulders, blanketing her blonde hair, and seeping into her black leather high-heeled boots, as if Mother Nature wanted to test Jenna's resolve. <u>To see whether a winter storm could derail her plans, and force her back to New York.</u>

Jenna kept forging forward. Really, what other choice did she have right now? If Jenna had one quality, it was that <u>ability to forge forward, to keep going when it seemed like all was lost.</u>

And right now, just about all was lost. <u>But she had a plan, and she'd get it all back.</u> Definitely.

A two-inch carpet of flakes covered the sidewalk as Jenna walked, under the swags of Christmas pine, past the crimson bows dotting the wrought iron lamp poles. Downtown Riverbend had already buttoned down for the night, with most of the specialty shops lining the street shuttered and dark. Only the café's windows glowed, like a beacon waiting at the far end of the white storm.

Jenna drew her coat tighter and dipped her chin to bury her nose in her blue cashmere scarf. She'd forgotten how cold winters got here. Forgot how the snow carried a fresh, crisp scent. Forgot what it was like to be in the small Indiana town that most people called heaven.

And Jenna had called prison.

The streets were empty, quiet, people safe at home and in bed. She was in Riverbend, after all, the kind of town where nothing bad ever happened.

Well, not nothing bad, but not *that* kind of bad. She was safe. Perfectly safe.

She increased her stride. Goodness, the snow seemed to have doubled in strength and depth in the twenty minutes it had taken her to buy a dozen cookies at the Joyful Creations Bakery. Even though she'd come in at closing time, the owner, Samantha MacGregor, had insisted on staying to fill Jenna's order—and then spending a few minutes over a cup of coffee getting caught up with her high school friend. Jenna had heard just about everything about everyone in town, even about people she wasn't so sure she wanted to be reminded of.

People like Stockton Grisham. He was here in town, Samantha said. "Returned a few years ago, and opened up a restaurant."

Stockton had returned to Riverbend? The last she'd known, he'd intended to wander the world, plying his culinary talents in some far-off location. He'd told her he wanted to make his mark on the world, one bouillabaisse at a time.

What was it about Riverbend that kept people coming back, or worse, encouraged them to never leave? Most days, Jenna was damned happy she had left.

Or thought she had been. For so many years, New York had been the only destination she wanted, the only address she imagined for herself. And now…

She increased her pace, shushing that persistent whisper of questions she didn't want to face. The snow blew and swirled around her but she kept going, her boots crunching on the icy crust forming over the snow. As she walked, sharp notes of ginger wafted up to tease at Jenna's senses, tempting her to eat one—just one—of the homemade windmill cookies.

She got into her car, laid the box of cookies on the passenger's seat and turned the key, waiting while the wipers brush off the coating of snow building up on the windshield. When the windshield was clear, Jenna put the auto into gear. The Taurus fishtailed a bit, protesting how quickly Jenna had pulled away from the curb. She pressed on the brakes. Took in a deep breath. It had been a long time since she'd driven in snow. In New York, she walked almost everywhere, cabbed or subwayed it for longer distances. Riverbend was no New York. There wasn't any public transportation or yellow taxis. Just her and the mounting snow—

And the job ahead of her.

She thought of turning back, of heading for the airport and retreating to her third-floor walk-up apartment in New York. Anything other than return to the town that had whispered about her life like it was an ongoing soap opera. She supposed, in many ways, it had been. But that had been years ago, and surely things were different now.

Jenna's hand hovered over the turning signal. Take a left? Or go straight?

Really, what was waiting for her if she turned left, and got back on that plane? Her only opportunities lay straight ahead, in this town she had tried so hard to leave behind, and now had become her only salvation. Riverbend, of all places. Jenna sighed and started driving.

If you noticed from the parts I underlined, Jenna's External Goal is rather vague, because I want the reader to keep turning the pages to find out what kind of salvation she needs and how she's going to get it. But it's clear she is there for something important, life changing. Her Internal Goal is clearer—she's seeking acceptance, retribution, and some self-healing (even if she isn't quite aware of that yet). Now, choose a book from your own shelf, and do a little analysis. What is the character's book-length External Goal? What is their book-length Internal Goal?

DOWNLOAD MY FREE HANDOUT

"The Highlighter Method of Learning to Plot" at JumpStartCreativeSolutions.com

CHAPTER TWO
KNOW THE WHY

If you did your homework in the previous chapter, then you know your Character's External Goal and maybe even a few Scene Goals that feed into the book-length Goal. Maybe you have started writing that big, important Scene, and although the pages are flowing, the Characters are acting and the Scene is moving forward, it all feels…flat. It just doesn't seem big enough or important enough, and you can't quite put your finger on why. Nothing's really working with what should be a fabulous Scene, even though it has a strong Goal at the heart of it. You think, *hey, I've got a great Goal here. What is the problem?*

Maybe the problem is a lack of Motivation. It can be a pretty common problem for writers when they are creating a Scene. They know what their Characters want, but not always do they know *Why*. Or the *Why* isn't important enough/big enough.

That's what Motivation is, in simplest terms—the *Why*. Motivation is the reason behind your Character's actions. Some people will figure out the main reasons (he wants to find the girl who needs a heart transplant and meet her because he's looking for worthy people to receive his organs, which is part of the plot of the movie *Seven Pounds*) but then they don't go deeper than that. You really need to be able to see inside your Character's head to understand the full reasons why they are acting the way they are and choosing the paths they take.

The deeper *Why* in *Seven Pounds* is that Will Smith's Character feels hugely responsible for a massive car wreck that killed several people. His actions resulted in deaths and the least he can do is give back his own life to make it right. Wow—now you really care, right? You can sympathize with him, even root for him as he embarks on his quest. His motivation is pure and deep and emotionally driven.

Most Character Motivations are about deep-seated emotional needs and wounds.

With *Shrek*, his Motivation to get his swamp back isn't just about the fairy tale creatures who have invaded because Lord Farquaad banished them. It's about his need for privacy and peace, because when he is in the world, people hate him and try to attack him, literally, with pitchforks. Shrek is rejected everywhere he goes because he is an ogre, and getting his swamp back is really about protecting his heart from more hurt.

Plan Deeper Layers

Great Motivation is what makes a show like *Lost* so interesting, and what made it such a huge hit. The writers did a lot of pre-planning before they started writing and they knew the Motivations for all of the Characters' actions. Those reasons weren't obvious in the Scenes, but you, as the viewer, *knew* there was more than they were showing. There'd be a word, an action, a reaction—something—that would clue you in to the fact that there was a lot more underlying the Characters' choices than what they were saying.

That's the thing with Motivation—you, as the author, should know all the reasons why Characters are doing something, but you don't necessarily have to show them all on the page. You can hint at the reasons, leave the reader guessing a little. Layer them in, and let the reader uncover the Character's layers with each page.

Make the Stakes High Enough

The best Motivations are also ones that we can all relate to and ones that have huge stakes for the Character (like saving the world or saving a loved one). It's hard to feel sympathy for a Character who wants to kill his neighbor because he wants to know what killing someone is like (well, unless you have a *Dexter* side yourself, but I'm wagering the majority of people don't). But you *can* feel sympathy for someone who wants to kill his neighbor because the neighbor is a child molester. That's the kind of visceral reaction we all can relate to. We wouldn't necessarily take the same actions, but we can understand it.

In *Disturbia*, for example, Shia LaBeouf's Character starts out merely curious about the neighbor next door. It's almost a game to find out if he's a killer. But things take a turn for the serious when the neighbor threatens Shia's mother. Shia loves his mother—she's all he has—and he will do whatever it takes, including kill the neighbor, to protect her. You can see his Motivations shift as the threat becomes personal.

As a side note, you'll see more references to movies than novels because chances are better that we have all seen the same movie than all read the same book. Plus, movies are great at Show, Not Tell, which we will get into later.

Creating the Motivation

As you are planning your book, do some thinking ahead of time to really look at what deep Motivations your Character could have for their Goals. Here are a few questions to get you started:

- What kind of Motivation would make your Character cheer on the most devious of plans?

- What Motivation would make your Character support a murderer?

- What Motivation would make your Character support a lie?

- What Motivation would make your Character support a robbery?

- What Motivation would make you do what your Character needs to do?

- What Motivation would make your Character face their Deepest Emotional Fears?

If you use these as a backdrop, you can come up with Motivations for nearly any Goal in a book. Bring it back to your personal choices and needs, and those of your close friends and family. Those are the universal truths (protecting family, protecting the innocent, saving a child, saving your own life) that we can all relate to and thus, support.

Make it Noble

You can make almost any Motivation work if you have a noble reason behind it. *Sophie's Choice* does this brilliantly. Her Goal seems horrible—choosing a child that she will send to his/her death. But the Motivation (to save one she must sacrifice the other, or they will kill both children) is so strong, the reader's heart is torn. You are invested in Sophie's decision from the very start.

In *Seven Pounds*, Will Smith puts the people he meets through a series of tests designed to be sure they are good people, the kind who will appreciate such a huge gift and sacrifice. For a large portion of the movie, we don't know why Will is doing this. We see his actions and know there is something more underlying each choice he makes. It takes almost the full movie to figure out all his reasons behind his actions. But there are hints, little gestures, reactions, and words that tell you this is hugely important to him.

Would that movie have worked as well if Will Smith's only reason behind finding organ recipients was because he had a surplus of organs in his Organs 'R Us warehouse? Or because he was fascinated by organ donation and wanted to explore how it impacts people?

I don't think so. The deeper Motivations of wanting to atone for the lives he took, of needing to feel worthy himself before he dies—all of this create a far more dramatic and compelling story. His Motivations are strong, they are noble, and even as we watch him take his own life, we are rooting for him and supporting him.

Any Goal Will Work—if Properly Motivated

You can make a Character do *anything*—kill his own wife to save his son (*The Box*)—as long as it's properly motivated. Sawyer in *Lost*, for example, wants to kill a man. At first, we aren't entirely sure why. We do know he killed one man in Australia—who turned out to be the wrong man—and we know he has this letter that he carries around everywhere. But as the story goes on, you find out that this man is the one who killed Sawyer's parents in front of him and ruined both their lives and Sawyer's life. You feel bad for the little boy in Sawyer, the one who watched his mother die, and you support his quest. But when he finally comes face to face with that evil man, he is torn. He's not a killer at heart, he's a con man with a soft spot. So the moment becomes a pivotal one for Sawyer— how badly does he want revenge, and in turn, to escape from the island?

When you are figuring out your Character's Motivation, dig deep to find out the emotional reasons behind their choices. We all make choices based on things that have happened to us in our pasts. The traumas, failures, risks…those are the things that shape us as humans. Think of Clarice, the FBI agent in *Silence of the Lambs.* Without her past and the slaughtering of the lambs, would she be as well suited for dealing with Hannibal Lecter? Her past creates in her a strong Motivation to save and rescue the innocent, and that forces her to overcome her fears and face Hannibal and his questions.

In short, Motivation is the *because* in a Scene. Multiple reasons why (multiple Motivations) can help deepen your Character and your Scene and is also closer to real life. In our own lives, our reasons for doing things often have layers of becauses behind the actions (we'll get into more of that later). The more those reasons can stem from deep-seated emotional needs, the more compelling your Scene will be.

Motivation is also a key factor in building the relationship between the reader and the Character, and when the reader is connected, they *care.* Most importantly, they don't put the book down, Instead, they rush to buy the next in the series, and tell their friends to do the same.

The Rule of Six

I have a cookie jar on my kitchen counter, and I have a bag of celery sticks in the refrigerator. At least a half dozen times a day, I wander into the kitchen for a snack, and although my Goal when I go in there is to eat healthy, and my Motivation is to stick to my diet, I end up grabbing the cookie. Well, for one, celery sticks are kinda gross, and cookies are the opposite of gross.

However, I am continually practicing the same self-defeating behavior. Over and over, I choose the treat that I know will push me further away from my goal. This, my friends, is why God invented therapy, so we can all figure out what drives us to choose cookies over celery and thus, defeat our own intentions.

When there aren't any therapists in the room, I like to do this thing (it's part of an online class I teach called The Rule of Six), where I find six reasons for something. I use it all the time when it comes to Motivation. Let me show you how it works—and how it can enrich Character Motivations in your books.

Let's play Rule of Six with this simple thing of cookie eating (and heck, maybe in doing this, I'll be better motivated to choose the celery sticks next time). Remember, the easiest way to figure out Motivation is to fill in the blank: WHY or BECAUSE. So, Shirley reaches for the cookie jar because:

Shirley's Six Motivations for Reaching for the Cookie Jar

1. Get something to eat

2. Satisfy my sweet tooth. That puppy is NEVER quiet

3. It's easier to grab the cookies than to wash the celery

4. Saw the kids with some, and felt justified that Mom should have them too

5. I had a really bad day. Bad review/argument/bills due/ fill in the blank

But the really deep one, the Motivation I don't think about at all, is the one that truly spurs my actions:

6. The longer I undermine my diet, the longer I can have the foods I love and avoid those icky ones. And avoid accountability for my actions.

Ding, ding, ding. It wasn't just about being hungry and satisfying a sweet tooth, now was it? Nor was it really about how difficult my day was. It's about how I don't want to take away my comfort foods, and if I have cookies in the afternoon, well, then, heck, I already blew the day, might as well have some at night. It's this subconscious thing. I don't do it on purpose. I'm in the kitchen, and I think to myself that I'm grabbing a cookie simply because I'm hungry. Yeah, it's way more than that as most things are.

We'll have a whole chapter on the Rule of Six, but if you want to do extra credit, try it right now. Find an action you commonly do, and list six reasons you do it.

The Why Isn't What the Character Thinks

Your Characters think they have one Motivation (or a couple). Get a loan to save Grandma's farm because it's in trouble, and that's where all her childhood memories are. Great Motivations, right? But if you go deeper and apply the Rule of Six, maybe you discover that the real reason your heroine wants to save Grandma's farm is because she is terrified to leave her small town in Iowa and find out she can't make it on her own. The farm is a security blanket, not just a roof over her head. In a book, Characters always—*always*—have deeper, buried Motivations that they don't know and you, the author, should.

That's the really cool thing about coming up with multiple Motivations. You can figure out some neat things about the Characters and start layering them in as you write. Hold on, cowboy. Don't just dump all those Motivations into the first Scene. You want your Characters to discover things about themselves and about each other as the book goes on, so if you're writing that dieting diary, you don't have the Character discover on page two that she's undermining herself. You save that epiphany for later. It's how it works in real life, and it should in your books, too.

A Mix of Internal and External

A lot of people ask me if I come up with six External and six Internal Motivations. To be honest, I'm the kind of writer who hates making Character charts and spreadsheets and lists that take more than one sheet of paper. I only come up with six Motivations total, and find that the first three are almost always external, and the last few (especially the last two) are the deeper Internal Motivations.

When you force yourself to go beyond the obvious External Motivations for a Character's actions, you find that depth. The best way to teach yourself how to do this is to take books and movies that you love and apply the Rule of Six in Motivations to them. Let's use one of the early Scenes in *Shrek*, for an example:

Shrek's Motivations for Going to Duloc

1. He wants to get the fairy tale creatures out of his swamp

2. He has to talk to Lord Farquaad in order to change the exile rule for fairy tale creatures

3. He is angry and outraged and helpless to fix this himself

4. He is finally fighting back against a world that hates him

5. The swamp is his sanctuary from bias and he needs that back

6. He wants more for his life, but is afraid to have it, and once he has a taste of it, he rejects it (Donkey and the fairy tale creatures) instead of embracing it, *so he doesn't get hurt*. Getting the swamp back keeps him in his safety zone physically and emotionally.

Did you catch that? *Shrek's deepest Motivation for pretty much everything he does is avoiding pain.* There are people who hate him so much, without knowing the person he is underneath the ogre body, that they want to stab him. They call him names, they shriek when they see him, they use him as a nightmare warning to their kids. Who wants to stay in a world that is so cruel? Shrek has learned to push people away before they can do the same to him. The fairy tale creatures aren't cruel to him (since they are also societal misfits) but he is so conditioned by his past that he is going to get rid of them too before they can hurt him. Deep down inside, though, Shrek is dying for acceptance and connection, but is terrified to have it.

Take a look at that list of Motivations and then start thinking about Shrek on a Scene-by-Scene basis. How did the writers layer in his Deepest Emotional Fears and Motivations? Do you see his actions and words from a slightly different perspective now?

If you go into your writing armed with this kind of deeper knowledge about your Character, then you can write a much more powerful book from the beginning. Deeper Motivations (and Conflicts, which we will talk about next) create complex Characters that readers really care about.

My second contracted book was a bear to write. The entire thing took place in an RV (*The Bachelor's Dare*, Silhouette Romance, December 2003, reissued as *The Beauty and the Bachelor*) and that made it really hard, Plot-wise, to figure out what Scene went where. They were all little vignettes, all in this same location (more on this in an upcoming chapter).

When I did Rule of Six, by figuring out the Goal for each Scene and then the Motivations, the entire book came together, wham, in an instant (if you read the book, there's a Scene in there where one of the Characters mentions a light bulb going off in his head...and that is the exact point where the light bulb went off for me with that book). If you are having trouble figuring out where Scenes are supposed to go or why a Scene isn't working, give this a try.

It Should Be Difficult

One other thing. When you do the Rule of Six, if you come up with six Motivations in less than six seconds, you're doing it wrong. It should be tougher the further down the list you go. You should be really searching and cursing my name and thinking there is no way there are six Motivations for this Character's actions. Keep digging, keep mining inside that Character's heart and you will find it. The deeper you go, the more you enrich your entire story.

A good book is like a rollercoaster, with the Scenes pulling the reader up that tense hill, then rushing for a second, then Tension, then rushing, then a moment of calm, etc. It's that stomach-in-your-shoes feeling just before the coaster reaches the top of the hill. Good books make you feel like that as you're reading and turning the pages so fast, dying to find out what happens next. When you have the Goals and Motivations moving along with the right pace, you'll easily build in that rollercoaster Tension.

Your Turn:

This time, I want you to list your Characters' Motivations. Bonus points if you list six and extra bonus points if you list six External Motivations and six Internal Motivations.

When you do this exercise, it should surprise you. You should be able to dig deep enough to find those diamonds that will bring your Characters to life and create a book that readers can't put down!

Scene Analysis

From *Beauty and the Bachelor*

In this scene, you can see Claire's motivation for wanting to win the RV (see the underlined parts):

Claire Richards ran her hand along the sleek exterior, the smooth metal gliding beneath her palm. If only men were this well-equipped. And this useful.

Her fingers slipped down the glossy surface, up and over the body ridges. Perfect. Absolutely perfect. Now all she had to do was win the forty-five-foot-long beast. She'd worry about wrangling it down the highway later.

The shadow of the massive cream and burgundy Deluxe Motor Homes RV dwarfed Claire, even though she was five-foot-nine. The house on wheels had plenty of space for the bedroom, kitchen and living room. Perfect, she repeated. A house and a getaway car all in one. She needed both—and the sooner the better. She'd made a promise and didn't have a lot of time left to keep it. Not nearly enough time.

But getting out of Mercy, Middle-of-Nowhere, Indiana, was about more than keeping a promise. No matter what, Claire was going to make the new start she needed. She'd given notice at the beauty shop, tucked most of her belongings into storage, and scraped up enough savings to fund her move. When Claire Richards leapt off a cliff, she did it without hesitation and without a safety net.

In the back of her mind, a tiny doubt whispered that changing her life was about more than physical distance. Claire quickly pushed the thought away.

The RV was her ticket to a new life in California and to the only family she had left. She gave the motor home a final pat, then crossed to the registration table.

"Is this where I sign up for a chance to win the RV?"

A cheerleader from Mercy High turned a clipboard toward Claire and handed her a pen. The girl had dark, bouncy hair and a thousand-watt smile that must have cost three dollars a watt at the orthodontist's. She wore a blue-and-white uniform and white sneakers. Change her hair to blond and she could have been Claire at that age.

"There's, like, a million people signed up and only, like, the first twenty get on." The girl gestured toward a board of rules. The number *20* shouted back at Claire, bold and big. "The contest starts Sunday. Try to be, like, early, and bring all your stuff." The cheerleader dipped her head and started filing her nails.

For a fleeting second, Claire felt like grabbing the girl's hand and telling her not to forgo a college education, not to put her faith in some silly boy who would end up working in the steel mill because his father worked there, and jobs were inherited along with the family cowlick. She wanted to tell Go-Team-Go Gidget to get out of Mercy while she still had a chance or she'd find herself still single at twenty-eight, <u>stuck in this town and desperate enough to sign up</u> for the September "Survive and Drive" contest at the mall.

<u>Hoping for the opportunity to win back the freedom and hope she'd had in abundance at eighteen.</u>

"Ma'am?"

That word jarred Claire back to reality. When had she gone from being a "miss" to a "ma'am"? Was there some road sign she'd missed? *You are now entering middle age. It's all downhill from here.*

CHAPTER THREE
CONFLICTS ARE NOT FISTFIGHTS

Conflict. Most of us try to avoid it, because no one really wants to be arguing with someone else or to have to confront a delicate situation. It's why you avoid your nosy, obnoxious, mow-the-lawn-at-six-in-the-morning neighbor at the block party, or why you don't talk to the woman who stole your boyfriend. I get it. I'm a Conflict avoider myself—but only in real life.

Books are another story. All books have Conflict and must have it, or the book falls flat and bores readers. Ironically, Conflict is also one of the things that writers struggle with, and often make too light or too easy to overcome. I think some authors are afraid to give their Characters any troubles (*but I like my protagonist! Why be mean to him and give him Conflicts?*). Or the Conflict is manufactured, and thus not true to the Characters.

If you remember this: *Conflict is the events, things, people, and emotional issues that stand in your Character's way,* then it becomes easier to pinpoint the Conflict in your story. Conflict is, at its essence, what prevents a Character from achieving his or her Goal, whether it's because of their own fears or outside events.

What Conflict is NOT:

An Argument: Your Characters can argue, of course, but good Conflict is not a disagreement that can be solved with a few quick words. The last thing people want to read about is other people fighting for an entire book. If one Character yells at another, they must have a strong and believable Motivation for doing so. It's not just fighting for fighting's sake.

A Delay: Conflict is not a wait in traffic or an alarm clock going off. That doesn't raise the stakes or increase the Tension, unless the wait in traffic is caused by the killer who is after your hero and wants to corner him so he can shoot him in the head. The ordinary frustrations that fill our days are not Conflict. They are simply frustrations, and they don't increase the Tension.

A Conversation that Needs to Be Had: That's called a conversational Conflict—meaning if the Characters just talk for two minutes, they'll clear things up. That can work for a Scene or two but if you carry it on too long, your reader begins to wonder what is wrong with a Character who can't ask that question he's dying to ask or that heroine who doesn't just tell the hero the truth. If the Characters are keeping information to themselves, they need to have a darn good reason—again, a *believable Motivation*—and there must be a cost to keeping that information secret. Meaning, things must get worse with every minute they keep their mouths shut. There are consequences to the decisions your Characters make.

What Conflict IS:

Affects Something Important to the Character: When something gets in your Character's way and stops them from reaching their Goals, it must be important. A man who is cut off from civilization by a snowstorm would be annoyed if he were going to miss a meeting, but if the stakes were higher and the snowstorm keeps him from reaching his stranded child, then the Conflict of being stuck becomes important. Then the reader cares and wants to see your hero figure a way out of that mess.

Stems from Issues in the Character Pasts: The best Conflict is created by the Characters themselves and their perceptions about the world. The woman who was abandoned as a child is going to have attachment issues, and thus, she won't be able to get close to or trust the one person she needs to. Dig deep into your Character's lives and figure out what makes them tick, what they are afraid of, and what has shaped their personalities. Use that to create Conflict tailored just to them.

Something that Forces Them to Change: We get out of the sun when it gets too hot. We put up an umbrella when the rain turns from mist to a torrential downpour. People don't change unless they are forced to, and Conflict is that catalyst to change. They must face their Deepest Emotional Fears, and overcome their greatest challenges, in order to attain what they truly want.

It's Always About Character: If you remember that Conflict comes *from* your Character, is what *drives* and/or *paralyzes* your Character, then you create a book that stems from Character, not from Plot. Plot-driven books are mostly about external forces on a Character, whereas Character-driven books are mostly based on the Internal workings of your Character. In turn, that creates a more emotional read, which draws the reader in and makes your book not only more compelling but more memorable.

It's Both Internal and External: That said, you want to be sure you have both Internal (emotional) and External (physical) Conflicts. A Character's fear of abandonment (Internal) will affect how she reacts when she is left alone at the wheel of a runaway train (the External).

It is in Opposition to the Character Goal: That opposition can, and should, come in many forms. Let's do an example to show you what I mean:

In *Sleepless in Seattle,* Annie starts out perfectly content with her life—or so she thinks. Her original Goal in the movie is to maintain status quo. When she's driving to Christmas with her family and fiancé, she overhears a radio show and realizes that the widower (Tom Hanks's Character, Sam) who is being reluctantly interviewed has had the kind of life she secretly dreams of. She becomes consumed with wanting to know more and uses her job as a reporter as an excuse to investigate (finding the truth about Sam becomes her new Goal). Annie, however, is a woman who has never let go of the rails on her life, never really taken a risk, and always done the sensible thing, including getting engaged to a man she finds dull. She is afraid to want more, because the jaded reporter side of her is convinced that "more" is fictional. Her Goal is to find and thus prove that this Sam guy isn't the charming, heroic widower he comes across as on the radio.

Internal Conflict: fear of risk, fear of failure,
disbelief in the fairy tale

External Conflict: Her job, her fiancé, the
miles between them

Annie has to confront and overcome both the Internal and External Conflicts to find her true happy ending. It's only when she takes a risk despite the possibility of failure that she finally finds true love.

In the best books, the Internal and External Conflicts are intertwined and impact each other. Annie's job gives her an excuse to investigate the man she heard on the radio, but it's also part of what keeps her in Baltimore. She takes one risk—writing Sam a letter—and then doesn't mail it at the last second. Her friend mails it for her, and when Annie gets his childish response (written by his son, unbeknownst to Sam), her belief that true love is fictional is reinforced. She retreats to the safety of her predictable, boring life, until she hears Sleepless in Seattle on the radio again.

But going after him, and after the longings of her heart, means letting go of her safety net and taking a risk. Every time she takes a chance (the letter, then flying to Seattle and seeing Sam with another woman), her Deepest Emotional Fears are reinforced. Those fears are what keep her from crossing the street when she's in Seattle and sees Sam. It's a visual of the crossroads she has in her mind and heart, and instead of going to the other side, she gets back in her car and flies home. In the end, her longing for the fairy tale she hears in Sam's voice drives her to end her relationship with her dull fiancé and take a giant risk—rushing through New York City to meet Sam at the top of the Empire State Building, à la the romantic *An Affair to Remember*. When he isn't there, she almost gives up, but the same curiosity that drove her to investigate Sam in the first place draws her to an abandoned backpack, and eventually, to Sam himself.

Each of Annie's actions are a tiny step out of her comfort zone. Her Conflicts and Deepest Emotional Fears make her retract and avoid. In the end, her External Goal of finding out the truth about this mysterious man and Internal Goal of finding the fairy tale love she's always longed for, empower her to take the biggest risk of all and show up on Valentine's Day. *Sleepless in Seattle* isn't a complicated Plot, but it does have those intricate layers of Conflicts that make for great stories.

Impossible Choices

If you want to create a book that's more layered and unpredictable, try to include Impossible Choices. These are the kind of decisions that put your Characters into a situation where no matter which decision they make, there will be huge repercussions. For example, in *A Tale of Two Cities,* Sydney Carton chooses to literally give up his life to save the people he loves, which means he will never be with them again (because he'll be…well, dead). It's a difficult, sacrificial choice that has been played out in many novels and movies after Dickens' famous take on the theme.

However, most of us don't write *A Tale of Two Cities* type books. We don't have stakes that are that high (where you have to choose to kill yourself or someone you love), but that's okay. We can have stakes that are *perceived* to be that high, and that is what will keep the reader reading. To do that, you need to start with one major concept:

Your External Goal, Motivation and Conflict should be in direct opposition to the Internal Goal, Motivation and Conflict.

Wait, what? How does that work? Direct opposition? It's actually a lot easier than you think to make this happen. Let's dissect *Pretty Woman* (one of my all-time favorite movies) using the GMC basics we talked about in previous chapter.

Edward (Richard Gere's Character)

External GMC:

Goal: To get through his trip to LA with few complications and *zero* relationship connections

Motivation: So he can concentrate on business and on his continual need to outdo his father; being a ruthless shark is all he knows; caring makes him soft and weak.

Conflict: He has social events where he needs a "partner." He also starts to like the owner of the company he is trying to destroy.

Internal GMC:

Goal: To be loved as he is

Motivation: He never measured up to anything anyone wanted from him

Conflict: In order to be loved as he is, he has to get close to people. Open his heart.

Be vulnerable. Shed his current identity. Form relationships.

Do you see how those are in direct opposition to each other? All Edward knows how to do is be cold, untouchable, wealthy, and successful. That's how he has gotten through life and dealt with being "very angry with his father." He hires a prostitute, because she is the epitome of no strings attached. Then he starts to care about her—and you know what he sees in Vivian? Himself, only in a different form. A woman who has been unloved and rejected. A woman who uses what she has to be successful. A woman who does everything she can to avoid getting close to people ("I do everything. But I don't kiss on the mouth.")

She is a kindred soul. She also doesn't want to get close to him, to believe that this fairy tale could come true. But she sees his vulnerabilities and sees the man he is, literally and figuratively, under his suit. She sees his heart. And she falls in love with him.

Over and over again, Edward is forced to decide—go for the jugular or go for love. He blows off work at her insistence, and literally takes off his shoes and tie and sets his briefcase and phone aside (being a normal man). He holds her at night, which opens his heart. He soothes her when she is treated badly. He rushes in as the hero when people are mean to her.

At the critical climax of the movie, Edward has to choose— his relationships or money/success. He astounds his team when he chooses to work with the owner of the company he is buying, instead of destroying it. But he lets Vivian go, because he isn't ready to open his heart yet. Then he realizes what that has cost him, and in a show of love and freedom from his old buttoned-up, straight-and-narrow persona, he makes a grand, public gesture of love and conquers (sort of) his fear of heights to go get her.

In *Pretty Woman,* virtually every Scene with Edward shows him being forced to choose between his External Goal and his Deepest Emotional Fears (which are the basis of his Internal Conflicts). It's the same with Vivian, but I only dissected Edward here. In your book, try to create a Plot that has that same structure of conflicting Internal and External Goals.

My advice for learning how to do this? Analyze *everything* you read and watch. List the External and Internal GMC. Are they in opposition? How did that impact the Plot? Your engagement as a reader/viewer? The story overall?

Tension vs. Conflict

Tension and Conflict are not the same thing, but work together, in a symbiotic relationship that keeps the reader glued to the page. It's a great way to get the most out of your Conflict because that Tension makes the reader care and worry about your Characters.

Conflict, as we've discussed before, is the roadblock, whether physical or emotional, that gets in your Character's way as he is trying to achieve his Goal. It's the villain chasing him with a gun, the car that won't start, the bank that won't give him the loan, his mistrust of people, his inability to get close to another person, etc.

Tension is the pit-of-your-gut feeling as you're reading a book that makes you keep turning the pages. It's the worry for the Characters. You worry whether they will be okay. Whether the hero and heroine will find love. Whether the protagonist will rescue his child. Whether the protagonist will find out the truth about her father, and if she does, what will happen then.

In short:

Conflict is the roadblock. Tension is the question.

Tension has two levels, something that Donald Maass talks about in *The Fire in Fiction*. There is macro-Tension—the big question. In other words, will the protagonist achieve his Goal? It's the question that runs from the beginning of the book to the end. Once that question is answered, the book is essentially done.

Micro-Tension is the second level. This is the Scene-by-Scene, paragraph-by-paragraph, sentence-by-sentence, word-by-word Tension. You use *all* the senses as often as possible to work this in. You use the dialogue, you use the descriptions, you use the pacing of the sentences. Study books that keep you feeling that Tension, that force you to turn the pages simply by the sheer *need to know*. In *Pretty Woman*, you can see that micro-Tension in Edward's face when he looks at Vivian. You can see it in that moment she whispers, "I love you," thinking he's asleep when he isn't.

That's micro-Tension. It's created using a lot of different techniques. Think about a horror movie and the Scene where the hapless heroine is ascending a dark staircase, approaching a slightly open door that creaks in the slight breeze coming in from the open window. Or is it creaking from something (or someone) else? That tense, tight, nervous feeling in the pit of your stomach as you watch the heroine climb those stairs, *knowing something bad is waiting for her*, is micro-Tension.

The director creates that by making the space dark, confined, putting the heroine at a physical disadvantage (no weapon, perhaps), and showing the emotions of trepidation on her face. He adds in the sounds coming from behind the door, the slight creak of someone walking across the floor, the feel of the cold door handle surprising the girl…in other words, he uses all the senses to create that Tension in the pit of the viewer's stomach.

Your Turn:

Get to know your Characters and their Deepest Emotional Fears. What are they most afraid of losing? Those are the emotions that create deep Conflicts. What is their deepest insecurity? What event in their past has brought them to this moment in time and these fears? Use those to create powerful Conflicts that create a connection between the reader and your book.

When you dig deep to get to know your Characters better, you can use that information to create fully formed people who must face their Deepest Emotional Fears in order to achieve their Goals.

Scene Analysis

Here's an excerpt from Dennis Lehane's *Gone, Baby, Gone*[1]. Look at how he uses the descriptions to create that Tension from the very first pages:

---

1   Dennis Lehane, *Gone Baby Gone* (New York, William Morrow & Company, 1998), 256.

Amanda McCready had been on this earth four years and seven months when she vanished. Her mother had put her to bed on Sunday night, checked in on her once around eight-thirty, and the next morning, shortly after nine, had looked in at Amanda's bed and seen nothing but sheets dented with the wrinkled impression of her daughter's body.

The clothes Helene McCready had laid out for her daughter—a pink T-shirt, denim shorts, pink socks, and white sneakers—were gone, as was Amanda's favorite doll, a blond-haired replica of a three-year-old that bore an eerie resemblance to its owner, and whom Amanda had named Pea. The room showed no sign of struggle.

The bedding, the pajamas, the missing doll...all that pulls at our heartstrings and increases the Tension about the missing girl. You feel her vulnerability, you worry for her, you wonder if she'll be found—and if she'll be alive when she is found. It creates Tension for the Characters, as well as the reader.

As I've said before, look at your Plot like a rollercoaster. There is Tension in the chug up the hill, when you know that terrifying drop is about to come. Your stomach is tight, you're nervous, you're holding on tight. *Click, click, click*, the wheels go up, your stomach gets into more knots. Then you hit the top, whiz down the terrifying hill, and then, for a few brief seconds, it's all flat coasting, before you start up the next hill. That's how Tension should work—rise and fall, rise and fall. If it's all tense, then that gets boring. You want to keep that roller coaster pace throughout.

You do that by using your Conflict tools. Throw roadblocks at your Characters. Let them conquer some of them, fail at others. Those moments of success create the flat parts of the roller coaster, and just when they think they're on a nice, even, quiet path, *wham*, you hit them with another roadblock/obstacle, i.e., Conflict. That creates even more questions—will the heroine be able to overcome this new problem and reach her Goal? Will she reach the top of the stairs before the killer catches her?

Conflict helps create Tension, and Tension helps add to Conflict. The more roadblocks and obstacles and Impossible Choices your Character has to overcome, the more the reader wonders if they can succeed at their Goal. Tension adds to the Conflict, because if the Character is fearful or doubting or anxious or torn between two decisions, it can make overcoming an obstacle that much harder. These two-story essentials have a strong symbiotic relationship that benefits both of them, because strong Conflict and strong Tension work well together. It's what keeps readers turning the page, dying to find out what happens next.

Bonus Scene Analysis

Here's an excerpt from *The Secret Ingredient of a Happy Marriage* where the Conflict is used in the Setting (the unfinished house), in the actions of the Characters (the suitcases), and in the unspoken things they don't say. Nora is conflicted about leaving, both Internally and Externally, something I show in the underlined parts:

> "Nora, let it go." He took out his phone. "I'll fix this."
>
> She snorted. Fix it? There was nothing he could do now. That yellow paper said it all. "I've heard you say that twelve thousand times, Ben. And all you've ever done is make it worse." Her gaze skipped over the kitchen, half painted, still missing three upper cabinets, a renovation started four years ago. Yet another of Ben's promises that had been broken the second the work got inconvenient. Once upon a time, she'd thought she could create a home here. Now some other family would stand on the front lawn, hold up a hand, and buy the house she loved for pennies on the dollar. Every memory she had, every mark on the wall for the kids, every fingerprint on the glass, would belong to someone else. "I'm going to pack some things and take the kids to my mom's until I find a better solution."

"You're leaving?"

"Yeah, Ben, I'm leaving. And I don't want to argue about it or cry about it. Let's just be adults here and admit we screwed this up. We"—she waved between them—" screwed us up. This whole thing with the house is a sign. We should go our separate ways and start over."

Silence. She'd finally spoken the words both of them had danced around for two years. Ben's gambling had taken a toll on their marriage, damage they'd never recovered from. He'd gone to rehab almost a year ago, thirty days of a desperate attempt to save his family. But the fractures only widened. It wasn't just the money he'd lost. Nora had watched him put a deck of cards or a roulette table ahead of their marriage, as if it were just another thing to gamble. The promises they'd made to each other on their wedding day became nothing more than words, and at some point, Nora simply stopped trying. They'd gone through the motions for the sake of the kids, but the death knell had sounded the night they'd moved into separate bedrooms.

Ben crossed his arms over his chest. "You're not taking my kids from me, Nora."

"You already did that yourself, Ben." She turned on her heel and walked out of the kitchen. If she stayed there for another second, her foolish heart would cave to the haunted look in his eyes, the pain etched in his forehead. How many times had she done that? How many times had she believed things would change?

All staying with him had done was cost her the only home her children had ever known. Cost her the family she'd wanted to build. The future she had dreamed of having. In the back of her bedroom closet, she found a trio of suitcases. She threw them open on the bed—the bed she had stopped sharing with her husband over a year ago—and started stuffing clean laundry inside. Enough for a few days. She'd figure out the rest later.

Ben leaned against the door, watching her for a long time without a word. Finally he said, "Don't go, Nora."

She hesitated at the hitch in his voice. The exposed wound in those words. *Stay,* some foolish, hopeful part of her whispered. *Stay and work this out.*

Instead she zipped the largest suitcase shut and then started filling the next one. "Why? Because there's something to save here? You and I both know there isn't."

"It's your birthday. We always go to dinner at Giovanni's on your birthday."

<u>Her hands stilled</u>, halfway through folding a Power Rangers T-shirt. "We *used* to go to Giovanni's, Ben. We haven't been in a long time."

"We went last year—"

"Last year, I spent my birthday driving to Foxwoods. You'd sold your car to some guy in the parking lot for five hundred bucks." <u>There was more, but she didn't say it</u>. Some secrets were better left in the past.

"I know I screwed up. A lot. But things have changed, Nora. *I've* changed."

She looked up at him, <u>into the eyes she'd once thought could see inside her soul</u>. At the face of the man she'd imagined growing old with, sitting on the back deck sipping wine as the sun set. "<u>You have. The trouble is, Ben, so have I</u>."

Also notice how much Conflict is in this short scene. The constant simmering Tension between them is what makes the reader turn the page, desperate to see if Nora and Ben work it out. There's a hundred Conflicts between them, both emotional (hurt) and physical (the house) but the Tension in the scene makes everything that much stronger. Nora is torn between saving her marriage and doing the right thing for her children; conflicted between the love she still feels for her husband and the need to get out of a situation that is only causing pain. She isn't one-dimensional, and neither is Ben, which is what hopefully makes the readers root for both Characters.

PART TWO
COMPELLING SCENES

CHAPTER FOUR
HOW SCENES WORK

We've talked about GMC, Character Weaknesses and Strengths, and finding their Worst Nightmare, all to create a strong Plot that will carry the entire book. A book, however, is made up of multiple Scenes, all of which feed into the overarching book Goal. If a Plot is an engine, the Scenes are all the parts that make the engine work (pistons, filters, transmission, hoses... and I have run out of engine parts I can actually name). All those parts work together to keep the engine moving. You can't just yank out a piston and keep the car running, right? It's the same with Scenes. Every single one of them should be so vital to the Plot that yanking it out wouldn't make the book run.

The components of Scenes are the same as the components of the overall book, just on a micro level (feeding into the macro level External and Internal Plots):

1. **An Author Goal:** This is what you, as the author, want the scene to accomplish. Basically, why are you writing this scene? Are you trying to show something specific about your character? Layer in some more emotion? Add some plot details?

2. **A Scene Goal**: That means something that the POV Character wants; something that feeds into the main Goal. Every single Scene should have an External and Internal Goal for the Point of View Character. Every. Single. Scene.

3. **Strong Motivation**: Whatever your Character wants, it has to be well motivated, or the reader will never buy it, just as with the overarching book-length Motivation

4. **Conflict**: These are the things that stand in the Character's way to achieving his/her Goal, and most of the time are part of the book-length Conflict

5. **Tension**: This is slightly different from Conflict. It's that ongoing twist in your gut feeling you get when you read the Scene, the kind of thing that keeps you on the edge of your seat and keeps you turning the pages

6. **Showing, Not Telling**: This is one of those concepts that takes a while to grasp, but once you get the hang of it, you'll see your writing transform. It's a powerful tool in storytelling (and we will get into it in detail later in this book)

7. **Things Go Wrong**: No matter what your Character's Goal is, and what the outcome is for that Goal within

the Scene, things have to get worse. Something has to go wrong, or the Character has to find out that success comes at a price. The minute everything is perfect is the minute the book is over, because you have lost your Conflict and Tension. More on how that works in a second

8. **A Well-Done Sequel**: The best Sequels are short and move you straight into action again. Sequels *do not* have to come at the end of the Scene—they can come at the beginning of the next one—but you need a Sequel somewhere

9. **A Hook**: The whole point is to get the reader to keep turning pages. That means you need to hook them and keep them hooked so that they stay up until the middle of the night, reading your book.

Let's take apart the first couple of Scene components. We'll get to Sequels, too, but bear with me for a second as I explain the basics.

Author Goals for a Scene

One of the things I hear often from writers is that they wrote a Scene just to have a funny moment because the book was too serious, or they wanted to show their Character's funny side. Or they wrote a sad Scene to add a moment of pathos. And my answer to that is—great, but that's not the only reason that Scene should exist. Remember what I said in the beginning? The reader is giving you *valuable hours of his time* to read your book. Don't waste that precious gift on scenes with no Plot value.

The Author's Goal for the Scene must dovetail with the Character's Goal for the scene. Yes, you, as the Author, should have a reason for writing the Scene, something you want to accomplish with it, like showing some humor or a moment of vulnerability in your Character. Be aware of your Author Goal for the Scene before you start writing because that helps you develop the course of actions that will comprise those pages.

For instance, if you want to show your Character in a moment of vulnerability, then you might throw them into a scary situation or one where all their skills are useless, and they have to depend on another to get them out of there. Or maybe take the tough-as-nails doctor (Gregory House) who never betrays an emotion, and have him operate on a pregnant woman (the episode "Fetal Position" in the show *House*). When the unborn child's finger curls around the doctor's, he can have that moment of vulnerability when he notices the fragility of life.

However, in doing this, your Character needs to be changed for either the good or bad (and their Scene Goal must be impacted, either positively or negatively). That moment of vulnerability can be a moment of weakness that makes it harder for the hero to stay focused, and maybe he makes a fatal mistake. The moment of humor can distract your heroine from her Goal of ripping the witness apart on the stand and she loses the case. Whatever the Scene Goal is, it must be one that feeds into the main Plot Goal at the time. It can't just be, *oh, look how sweet she is with that lost kitten.* There has to be more to the Scene so that it has a purpose within the book.

Sit down before you write your Scene and decide what you want to show the reader. Having your Author Goal determined beforehand can be really helpful when you move onto the other parts of the Scene. Ask yourself the following:

1. What do you want to accomplish in this Scene?

2. How will doing this change your reader's perception of your Character?

3. How will doing this increase the Tension?

4. How can you accomplish your Goals while also Showing, not Telling, and using action instead of passive events?

Character Goals for a Scene

I'm going to repeat this here for those of you in the back who were passing notes instead of paying attention (just kidding). *Your Author Goal has to feed into the Character Goal and both of those have to feed into the overall book story arc.* That means they are stepping stones to get the Character from A to B in the book. Every time your Character shows up on the page and the reader is in his Point of View, he *must* have a Goal for being there.

Your Characters need a Goal for every single Scene.

Don't waste any time on the page, kids. Scenes are about action, about increasing the Tension and raising the Stakes, and making the reader flip those pages so quickly it's as if they're on fire. In the above example, House is saving the baby's life (and the mom's). His Scene Goal is to determine the best course of action to save the mom because, in his words, the mom can always have another baby. In his callous mind, he's going to let the baby die. Then this moment with the baby's hand takes him by surprise. House works very hard to never betray emotion, to never admit he's wrong, and this moment leaves him so stunned, he pauses and the patient goes downhill. He has to spring into action and set his emotions aside again, which is his comfort zone (if House actually grew a heart like the Grinch, the series would end). It's also a moment evocative of how Gregory House is starting to fall apart, something Cuddy (his boss) has noticed, which has her ordering him to take a vacation. The audience knows he needs the vacation, and this moment of vulnerability shows a Weakness in House's armor. It endears him a little more, even as he goes back to his Vicodin/alcohol-fueled miserable self.

As I have said before, all the Character Scene Goals should feed into their overall book-length Goal. Whatever they want to achieve/get before the end of the book, the Scene Goals should be a part of that arc. For example, if a Character wants to rescue his kidnapped family, then each Scene will have a Goal that gets him one step closer to rescue. Whether it's contacting the police, or making the ransom drop, or uncovering a clue…etc. Those Scenes create the actions that are your Character Goals.

Some writers make the Goals too tame, or too easy to achieve. If your Character only needs to walk across the street to find his missing kid, that's not a tough Goal. That isn't the kind of Goal that takes many pages of a book to accomplish.

Those Scene Goals need Conflicts and Motivations, both Internal and External, just like the Plot does. Every single Scene is a mini-plot, filled with all the same elements we have talked about up to this point. Layering in Conflict and Motivation, especially Internal, means you also layer in lots and lots of emotion. And what does emotion give you? All together now—a compelling book.

It's all about continually ramping up the action and Tension for your Characters, so they must work hard to reach that pinnacle. Each of these Scene Goals should include roadblocks and enemies and setbacks. At the end of the book, after all these mini-Goals, the Character might achieve their Goal, but at a price (like the hero rescues his son but loses his best friend in the process). Those are the kind of impossible situations that make for a compelling read and really bring the story to life.

Ask yourself almost the same questions with the Character Goal as you did for the author Goal:

1. What do you (the Point of View Character) want in this Scene?
2. Why? What is so important about achieving this Goal?
3. What will you sacrifice in order to obtain this Goal?
4. What actions are you going to take to achieve your Goal?

In the example with House, the last thing he wanted in that episode was to feel for the baby. To him, it was a very clear medical decision—save mom or save baby. He thought the mom should sacrifice the baby and when the baby touches his hand, it touches his heart. For a doctor who makes it a rule not to get emotionally involved in a case, this moment dramatically increases the Tension.

You can have a small moment like that or a much bigger one (best friend dying while kid is saved). That doesn't matter— what does matter is that at the end of the Scene, the Tension is tighter, the Stakes are higher, and the Character is faced with more Conflict. The minute you lose your Conflict is the minute you lose the page-turning appeal. And in the process, lose the reader.

Your Turn:

Go through your book and for every single Scene, write down your Point of View Character's Goal for that Scene, both External and Internal. Bonus points for finding the Motivation and Conflicts, too. If you don't have a Goal, build one in—and make sure it somehow affects the book-length Plot arc.

Scene Analysis

From *Really Something*

(A little backstory here—Katie is Duncan's sister (Duncan is the hero) and she's paralyzed from the waist down. She's an angry girl, whom Duncan has nearly given up on being able to reach emotionally. Allie is the heroine, who has returned to Tempest, looking 180-degrees different from when she was there as a girl, and is finding herself wrapped up with Duncan all over again, even though he doesn't know who she really is. Duncan hired her to sit with his sister because the regular helper quit.) In this excerpt, I want you to look for the scene goal for Katie. How does this feed into the book-length goal of Allie wanting to prove herself as a location scout and get a little revenge on Duncan at the same time? How does Allie find herself conflicted, both in her external and internal goals?

> Allie left the room but stood outside the door. Inside, Katie cursed, grumbled several unflattering things about Allie. Then, finally, Allie heard the sounds of her slipping into the clothes, with a few more curses thrown in. "I'm ready now, Nurse Ratched."
>
> Allie returned to the room. Katie had exchanged her nightgown for the yellow summer dress, its pale color making her skin seem more vibrant, particularly against her dark hair, which Allie noticed hung limp and slightly tangled against her

shoulders. "Let's brush your hair," Allie said, rising to retrieve Katie's brush and hand mirror from her dresser. "Make a whole beauty day of it."

"I don't want to. Who's gonna care what I look like?"

"You."

Katie shook her head. "I stopped caring a long time ago."

Allie curled her palm around the soft boar's hair bristles. Katie had a hell of a wall up, and every time Allie thought they'd taken out a brick, Duncan's younger sister threw another one in its place. Time to pull out her personal sledgehammer and start knocking a few of those down. She couldn't leave Katie like this, couldn't return to L.A. knowing the girl was still in this bed. "Do you know I went on my first date when I was twenty-two?"

"Bullshit."

Allie drew a finger under Katie's chin, waiting until the girl's wide blue eyes met her own. "I'm serious. When I was younger and overweight, I didn't have boyfriends. I was only asked out once and I think," Allie drew in a breath, surprised that the thoughts pained her still, "he only did it to get a laugh out of his friends."

"What kind of loser does that?"

Your brother. The one guy I thought was different from all the rest. Allie shook off the thought and pasted a bright smile on her face. "Anyway, all I'm trying to say is that things can change. *You* can change."

Katie was quiet for a long while, then she reached for the hand mirror and traced a circle along the plastic rim. "I used to do this, you know. Worry about my appearance. I invested in more Revlon than RuPaul."

Allie laughed. "So you do have a funny bone."

"I used to." Katie sighed. "I used to have a lot of things."

Allie's hand covered Katie's. "And you can again. You have a lot of gifts, Katie Henry, but they're going to waste in this room." Allie swiped at her eyes and saw Katie do the same, then the two of them shared a laugh that erased the emotional moment. "Come on, let's brush your hair. Put on some lip gloss."

"That's not much of a beauty day," Katie said, brightening finally, a smile curving across her lips, her eyes glistening as they met Allie's, the sadness giving way to a tiny sparkle of hope. "A true beauty day is when you paint your nails some ungodly bright color and pluck your eyebrows and try on really bad eye shadow."

"Then that's what we'll do." Allie retrieved her purse from downstairs, then dumped the contents onto Katie's bed. Three bottles of nail polish tumbled onto the comforter. "Pick a color."

A grin curved over Katie's face. "Red, of course. Because I'm a bad girl."

Allie laughed. "Red it is." She slid down to the end of the bed and moved the blanket aside. "Okay. Toes first."

Katie shook her head so hard, her hair whipped across her cheeks. "No."

"I can't do your hands first," Allie explained. "You won't be able to brush your hair or do your makeup."

"Don't waste your time on those," Katie said, indicating her feet with an angry flick of her wrist. "They're useless and ugly."

Allie put a hand on Katie's bare, pale foot, not because she thought the girl might feel the touch, but to show her that her paralysis didn't disgust or repel her. "You're still a girl, Katie, regardless of what happened to you. And a girl paints her toenails." Before Katie could protest, Allie had twisted the top off the bottle of OPI and began applying the vibrant cranberry color.

Katie got busy brushing her hair, at first with quick, angry strokes, then with shorter, slower ones, her face turned away as though she didn't care what color her toes were.

But out of the corner of her eye, Allie saw a tear slip down Katie's cheek, puddling in the dimple of her smile.

DOWNLOAD MY FREE HANDOUT
"The Highlighter Method of Learning to Plot" at JumpStartCreativeSolutions.com

CHAPTER FIVE
LET'S MAKE A SCENE

A Scene has two parts to it—the Scene itself and the Sequel, which is the Character dealing with the results of the Scene. Just as the Plot framework has structure, so too does the Scene framework. Once you understand structure, Plotting becomes much easier because the skeleton of the book becomes logical and definable. Note I didn't say you should have a rigid structure—books are fluid and dynamic, and their Plots should be, too. All books, regardless of genre, have some kind of structure, and Scene and Sequel form the building blocks of that frame. Think of Scenes like Legos that you can take apart and put back together, always interlocking, but stacking in new ways each time to create your masterpiece.

Jack Bickham, author of *Scene and Structure,* one of my favorite books on writing, said, "Most successful fiction today is based on a structure that uses a series of scenes that interconnect in a very clear way to form a long narrative with linear development from the posing of the story question at the outset to the answering of that question of the climax."[2] Basically, Scenes form the daisy chain of the Plot, interlocking from beginning to end.

It All Starts with Goals

As we just discussed, every single Scene has a Goal that feeds into the overarching book Goals (both External and Internal). For example, if Jane wants to find her missing husband, she's going to take several steps (Scene Goals) to retrace his last steps and find out where he is now. There are no unnecessary Scenes, and no Scenes that waste the reader's time. Jane's not going to stop in the middle of her search for her beloved husband to go shoe shopping, or for free donut day at Dunkin'. She's going to keep moving along the trajectory of steps that lead to her book-length Goal, right up until the story is resolved.

If you can't name the Point of View Character's Goal for every single Scene, then it's time to go back and work on the structure. Nine times out of ten, if you have a book that feels flat or stuck in the middle, or that starts trailing off into nothing, chances are good the problem is going to be found in the Scene Goals and how the Sequels are impacting the Stakes.

---

2   Jack Bickham, *Scene and Structure* (Cincinnati, F&W Media, 1993), 176.

How do you fix that? By creating *failure*. When Characters fail, in some way shape or form, things get worse, and it forces Internal change on the Character. Failure is a type of Conflict, and Conflict makes for interesting books.

How Scene and Sequel Works

Let's take our imaginary Jane and her missing hubby to illustrate Scene and Sequel. In a Scene halfway through the book, her Goal is to try to do a geolocate on the last photo sent by her husband. She starts off great, hiring a tech whiz friend who knows how to get that kind of information from a photo.

She gets the photo, the tech whiz friend unearths a hidden geolocation tag (and I'm totally making this up because I am no tech whiz), so Jane thinks success! She's that much closer to her Goal. *But...*

And this is where the power of Scene and Sequel comes into play. That tiny little word changes everything and creates that pit-of-your-stomach Tension that keeps you reading the book until long after midnight. She gets her Goal, but...

What now? the reader thinks. *How can things get worse for poor Jane? I can't wait to keep reading and see how this turns out!*

The but is a powerful tool in fiction. It's what keeps the reader on tenterhooks. She keeps reading, desperate to see the resolution. The but is also part of the Failure in the Scene.

Here's the secret to Plots with great Tension:

Whether your Character achieves his Goal or not, things must get worse.

Failure is things getting worse (there are different kinds of Failure, which we'll get to in a second). Failure propels the Plot and keeps the story engine moving forward. That's the key to escalating Stakes—ending your Scenes with things getting worse in some way. Maybe Jane tries the geolocate thing but it doesn't work, and what's worse, she finds out that her husband's phone doesn't belong to him at all, but to some mystery woman. Now her Goal of finding him just got infinitely more difficult.

When you get to the end of the Scene, you should be able to answer the question: *Did the Character get what they wanted?* with one of the following answers:

a. **Yes, but...** Yes, the Character achieved his or her Goal, but at a price that is too high or difficult to pay. For example, Jane finds her husband, but must sacrifice her best friend to rescue him.

b. **No, and furthermore...** This is when the Character doesn't achieve his Goal and things get even worse. Not only does the heroine not get the loan to save the family farm, but she returns home and finds out a fire has wiped out her entire crop and killed her handyman.

This spirals her into more trouble and takes the Plot into new directions.

What these answers do is give you new twists on your Plot, which creates more interesting stories and more Tension.

If you're a bit confused, hey, that's okay. Let me break it down a bit more:

The Scene is the actions the Character takes to get closer to the Goal and the Sequel deals with the reaction to what happens in the Scene.

In other words, the *Sequel is the aftermath*. In the days of Dickens, Sequels were often as long as the Scenes themselves with pages and pages of the Characters thinking and planning and thinking some more. Today's reader doesn't have time for long, introspective passages. They also don't want to read about people thinking for hours (have you ever watched someone think? It's boring as hell), so make sure your Sequel is active. Sequels should be short and comprised of four elements:

1. **The emotional reaction:** Are they feeling disappointment, sadness, grief, joy, fear, anger? How does your Character feel about what just happened?

2. **The Quandary**: This is a new question for the Character, essentially, "What am I going to do now?"

3. **The Decision:** The Character makes a plan (remember, no one wants wimps for protagonists, so your Character should make a plan). For instance, after finding a link to the mystery woman with her husband's number, Jane takes off to confront her.

4. **The Action:** This is your next Scene. The Character has made a decision; now he needs to take action and move forward. This leads to a new Goal, a new Scene and so on and so forth. See? Interlocking Legos.

In simplest terms, **Scene** *and* **Sequel** *is* **Action** *and* **Reaction.**

Those four parts are what creates this lovely daisy chain for a Plot. Character goes after Goal, things get worse, Character creates a new plan of action, which becomes the next Scene Goal, and so on and so forth, until everything is resolved (and the book is over).

Sequels are typically put at the end of Scenes, but there is no hard and fast rule that says it has to go there. If your Scene ends with the butler being shot, that's a fabulous hook that will be muddied by the Sequel. You can open the next Scene with the Sequel and keep it to a couple of lines so the reader knows the Motivation behind the new Scene Goal.

Don't Forget the Internal Plot

When your Character is going after his or her external Goals, there should also be some kind of Internal Goal for the Scene. The Character may or may not be aware of this Internal Goal, but you as the author should know. Poor Jane with the missing husband might be trying to ease her guilt about going away for a girls' weekend just before dear Hubby disappears. Or maybe she's trying to overcome her fear of failure for not being a good spouse, or losing her job and putting huge financial stress on the family.

However, the Scene conclusion should also impact the Character emotionally (because this is what forces them to grow emotionally by the end of the book). If Jane makes things worse and doesn't get the geolocation, maybe that quadruples her feelings of failure, and she must overcome that paralyzing fear in order to take the next step.

Your Turn:

Look at a troublesome Scene in your book. Write down your Character's External and Internal Goal, Motivation, and Conflict. Then look at the ending of the Scene. Did they achieve their Goal? How did things get worse? And if none of that is happening, then how can you rewrite to up the stakes?

Scene Analysis

I took an excerpt from the first chapter of Marcus Sakey's *The Blade Itself*[3] to show you Scene and Sequel in action:

Opening:

> The alley wasn't as dark as Danny would've liked, and Evan was driving him crazy, spinning the snub-nose like a cowboy in some Sunday matinee. "Would you put that away?"
>
> "Keeps me cool." Evan smiled the bar-fight grin that showed his chipped tooth.
>
> "I don't care if it makes you feel like Rick James. You shouldn't have brought it." Danny stared until his partner sighed and tucked the pistol into the back of his belt. Evan had always lived for the thrill of the job, all the way back to when they had stolen forties of Mickeys from the 7-Eleven. But the addition of the gun made Danny uneasy. Made him wonder if Karen was right to suggest he start thinking long-term. Reconsider his options.

Danny's Goal for the Scene is to get through this robbery without any additional problems. He's realizing that

---

3   Marcus Sakey, *The Blade Itself* (New York, St. Martin's Press, 2007), 320.

he doesn't want to do this anymore, and maybe should think about becoming something other than a criminal.

Danny and Evan are initially successful with the robbery, *but...*

Sequel/End of Scene:

For a hesitant second nothing happened.

Then Evan exploded. Whatever demons shooting the pawnshop owner had freed took control of him again. He raised his pistol and pulled the trigger, aiming in a triangle of quick blasts. Not pointing at the lock but trying to hit her, trying to kill. At Danny's feet, the man groaned. Evan frothed and raged, kicking the door again. The frame was cracking, and Danny thought he could hear a whimper behind it. Everything had gone crazy, he was standing beside a pool of blood, Evan making enough noise to pull people for blocks, the lights on, for Christ's sake, the &%^$# lights on.

Danny had taken two falls, one county and one state, done the time like a man, but for this they'd get *years*.

No. No more.

He opened the front door and slipped out into the night. His body screamed to run, just go, but he made himself walk. Not draw attention. Just a guy headed for the El, nothing noteworthy about that.

When he was two blocks away, he heard the sirens.

So what happened here? Things got way worse—a man gets shot and Evan is freaking out and drawing attention. Danny is in danger of going back to prison. His reaction is found in the last part of the paragraph when things go south: *the lights on, for Christ's sake, the &%^$# lights on.*

His quandary is whether to stay or go. He's there with his friend and things have not gone well. His decision is quick because things are spiraling out of control, and he doesn't have time to dither: *No. No more.* His new action is to slip out the door and walk away. The Sequel is *active*, not passive, and creates a brand-new action and increased Tension. That builds the suspense and is part of what made Sakey's debut novel a breakout success.

CHAPTER SIX
FIVE PLOT KILLERS

When you go to look at a house in a brand-new subdivision, very often there's the base model, which has all the stuff you need in a house—walls, roof, appliances, floors. But then you stop by the model house, the one with the granite countertops and voice-activated faucets and wood plank floors. That's the fancy one, with all the bells and whistles, and the one that you remember. Scenes and Plots are kind of like that. You've got your basic author builder's model, and then there's the unforgettable, impactful deluxe version.

If you want a Plot that goes to the next level, you've got to work a little harder on your Scenes and make every single one important. Let's talk about five issues that DRIVE your readers crazy, and then talk about how to ramp up the Scenes to make them into something more exciting.

D: The Disjointed Plot

A Disjointed Plot is episodic (and if you've heard that comment from editors or readers, chances are your Plot is suffering from disjointedness). Common signs and symptoms of a Disjointed Plot are:

1. Lots of things are happening, but...

2. Each Scene can stand alone

3. There is no connective thread to the plot

4. The stakes do not rise progressively in each Scene

5. There is little to no emotional growth for the characters

What a Disjointed Plot boils down to is a whole lot of Scenes that have nothing to really connect them to each other. My second book, as I mentioned previously, had this problem. I didn't have a strong overarching External Goal for the main characters that could create a series of logical events and steps that fed into the External Goal (i.e., Scenes).

If you are finding that your plot lacks cohesion, then the cure is to find a strong External Goal, one powerful enough that the reader will root for your character to achieve it, and a strong emotional reason behind that goal. For instance, in *A Quiet Place*, Emily Blunt and John Krasinski don't just have to survive against the noise-sensing monsters, they have to protect their children who were tremendously traumatized by the death of one of their siblings. And they have a baby to protect, a baby who will be part of this new world going forward, and a baby that symbolizes a new start for this family that has suffered so much. We are rooting for them from the first scene. Every step the family takes moves them closer to their ultimate External Goal of finding a safe place for their family and the new (noisy!) baby.

When I wrote my second book, I got stuck about a third of the way into the book and realized it was partly because my Characters didn't have Scene Goals. The story was episodic, meaning that each of the Scenes was an episode in that Character's life, but the Scenes didn't string together to support the bigger book-length Plot. To fix this, I went back through every Scene and listed my Character's Goal for that Scene, along with their Motivation and Conflict.

It made all the difference in the world. Suddenly a static book (which was also static physically because the Characters remained in the same small location for most of the book), became dynamic, with Increasing Stakes and increased Tension.

R: The Routine Plot

A Routine Plot is predictable. You know what's coming before you turn the page. When that happens, the reader gets bored and very often, stops reading. Common signs and symptoms of a Routine Plot are:

1. The reader can accurately predict the character's next move
2. There are few to zero twists and turns
3. The plot has been done before a hundred times
4. The stakes rise, but in a predictable way
5. There is little to no emotional growth for the character.

Frankly, I think life is too short for boring books and movies. I stop reading or watching the minute I've figured out the Character's next moves. Think about the last book you read that was so predictable, you didn't even bother turning to the next chapter. You didn't care what happened, because the Character didn't have a lot of emotional investment in their Goal, and the journey to achieve the Goal was ho-hum and predictable.

I: The Indecisive Plot

The Indecisive Plot suffers from the infamous "Murky Middle" where the book just kind of wanders around in a circle, mumbling to itself, and bumping into the walls. Some common signs and symptoms of an Indecisive Plot are:

1. You're stuck. Period.
2. The plot isn't changing
3. Things aren't progressively getting worse
4. The stakes aren't rising
5. There is little to no emotional growth of the character.

The reason you have a Murky Middle goes right back to not having a strong enough Goal, Motivation, and Conflict. The Goal simply isn't important enough. Remember when we talked about examples of boring Goals? Things like needing a new pencil (okay, so that's an extreme example) or needing to move or get a promotion or build a fence aren't big Goals. Unless, of course, there are huge and emotional Motivations behind those Goals. If your Character needs to move because her child is being stalked by a serial killer, that's a strong Motivation. If your Character needs a promotion because he has wiped out the family savings on a pyramid scheme and now his kid needs a kidney, that's a strong Motivation.

In order to cure the Indecisive Plot, you have to throw in some surprises, too. When you get to that Murky Middle, that's when you take the Plot left instead of right. Meaning, you throw in an unexpected Twist. What if the dad who wiped out the family's savings finds a million dollars in a briefcase, and just as he's heading to the hospital to pay for his child's kidney surgery, he's kidnapped by the bad guys? Or worse, what if his child is kidnapped right out of the hospital? Or maybe the dad sacrifices everything he has to get the money for the surgery, only to find out that the whole diseased kidney was a scam created by a vengeful ex-wife? Twists and Turns are what keep your reader on her toes. Developing them requires some out-of-the-box thinking, so that you're not choosing to use a Twist that's as routine as an alarm clock.

V: The Victim-Based Plot

The Victim-Based Plot is a "Perils of Pauline" kind of story. Everything is being done to the character, and they are a continual victim. They're the kind of people the reader thinks is TSTL (Too Stupid to Live) because they only whine and react, instead of taking the bull by the horns. Some common signs and symptoms of the Victim-Based Plot are:

1. The main character does not act
2. There's a lot of whining and agonizing
3. There is an outside force or character driving all the action
4. Main character is always in reaction mode
5. The stakes aren't rising
6. There is little to no emotional growth of the main characters

I bet you're starting to see a common thread to these BTDT Plots—a lack of emotional growth. Static Characters, who never change or grow, or get challenged emotionally, are boring to read about. We *want* to see Characters learn those tough lessons. We want to see them become the best versions of themselves. We want to see them tackle their demons. So make them do that in your book.

E: The Emotionless Plot

The Emotionless Plot comes from a lack of emotional connection between the reader and the characters. Emotion, as I have said probably way too many times, is the key to a compelling novel. Readers will forgive pretty much anything if your book grabs them emotionally. Fiction readers want to be sucked into your imaginary world. They want to know and love your Characters. The only way to do that is to build an emotional connection. An Emotionless Plot is characterized by:

1. There are few, if any, teary moments in the book
2. The reader doesn't care about the characters or the outcome
3. The characters are forgettable
4. The stakes don't rise internally
5. There is no emotional growth on the part of the main characters

When a book is emotionless, no one cares how it ends. No one remembers the Characters or tells their friends about it. I recently read a book that was adapted from a screenplay. The author (who had originally written it as a screenplay that didn't sell) basically just added some descriptions to the book and called it a novel. The Plot was one that could have had a ton of emotion, but instead it was meh. It didn't grab me and wasn't the kind of book that I wanted to stay up late reading because I simply didn't care.

The types of Plots I talked about above are pretty common. Even though everyone knows you need a Plot, you'd be surprised how many books I have seen in my work as a content editor and author coach that have no Plot or a very weak Plot. The writer thinks they have a Plot, when in reality, what's on the page is two Characters who are being *acted upon* instead of doing all the acting. Or the Characters are flat and dull, with no real emotional growth.

DRIVE-type Plots tend to have pages full of thinking and reacting, and not a lot of action. When Characters are doing a lot of thinking, there's not a hell of a lot of Plot. Plain and simple.

Your Plot, remember, is the engine that propels the book forward. If you put cheap gas in your car or don't remember to change the oil, it's not going to perform at its best. You might have all the right parts in the engine but it's still churning along in the slow lane.

Create Increasing Stakes

One of the keys to a next-level Plot is to always have Increasing Stakes. As the book progresses, things must keep getting worse, and in a next-level book, it seems like everything is getting worse and the Characters are in impossible-to-escape situations, both Externally and Internally. These are the books with huge moral decisions and end-of-the-world scenarios.

Even in a regular Plot, you need to continually ramp up the stakes. When things are happy and smooth, the Characters become boring, and the reader loses interest. Think about it this way: If your neighbor Bob comes over every morning for coffee, and on Monday, he says, "I think someone's embezzling money out of my company," you'd think *hmm...that's intriguing.* On Tuesday, he says, "My accountant has gone missing." Even more interesting. On Wednesday, he says, "Now my wife is gone. There's a trail of blood in the garage."

Whoa, what? As soon as he says that, you'll be dragging out the Cinnabons and begging Bob to stay and tell you more, right? Imagine Bob comes over on Monday and says, "I think someone's embezzling money out of my company." Then on Tuesday he says, "False alarm, it was just an accounting error." And Wednesday he says, "My wife and I are so happy. My business is running great. Oh, and let me tell you about the garden and how great my tomato plants are doing..."

Which intrigues you more? Which gets you thinking? Which keeps you up at night? Which scenario brings out the good pastries?

When the stakes keep getting higher, things are getting worse for your Character, and if the reader has bonded with that Character, they are going to keep reading to see if things work out. Increasing stakes also forces the Character to act, which creates a more active Plot, and keeps the reader engaged.

How do you increase the stakes? Glad you asked. First, as we previously discussed, you must have a Plot with a strong External and Internal Goal, Motivation, and Conflict. Let's delve into that a bit more:

1. **The GMC has to be something that matters to the Character, and thus matters to the reader.** In *Shrek*, for example, he starts out wanting privacy, but that is taken away early on by Lord Farquaad when he dumps the fairy tale creatures into Shrek's swamp. Shrek needs his privacy, not just to take mud baths, but to protect him (literally and figuratively) from the slings and arrows of the world.

2. **When the GMC matters to the Character, they will go to great lengths to achieve it.** Shrek's great lengths aren't the same great lengths that Liam Neeson goes to in the movie *Taken*, but they are huge for his Character. Shrek faces the very world that despises him, and interacts with people who make him miserable, all to get his swamp back.

3. **The GMC is relatable and thus, important to the reader, too.** We can all relate to being hurt or ostracized (*Shrek*). We can all relate to every parent's Worst Nightmare of having their child kidnapped (*Taken*). We can all relate to losing love (*Romeo and Juliet*). Those relatable situations trigger emotions that give the reader something to latch onto, which creates an emotional bond with the Character.

4. **Things must keep getting worse to create a Black Moment.** The Black Moment in a book is when all is lost, and hope dies for the Characters (and the reader). In *Shrek*, that Black Moment is when he enters the church, and it's too late—Fiona is already legally married. In *Taken*, it's when Liam Neeson finds his daughter—but she's being auctioned off to a man who is buying her virginity, and there are a lot of bad guys in the way to save her.

5. **The Black Moment shows how much the Character is willing to risk to get what matters most.** Note I didn't say to achieve their Goal. Sometimes, the Character realizes in the Black Moment that what matters most to them isn't what they thought they wanted. When Shrek is in that church, he realizes he wants Fiona more than he wants privacy.

Weaknesses and Strengths

Everyone has Weaknesses and Strengths. I'm a bit of a procrastinator, but I'm also a super-fast writer, which is what allows me to pull a deadline out of the fire at the last minute. Those Weaknesses, however, can bite me in the butt if I'm not careful, and cause all kinds of problems. That's exactly how it should work in your book for your Characters, only on a bigger scale.

If you take nothing else from this chapter, remember this:

The Characters' Weaknesses will get them into trouble, over and over again, and their Strengths are what will save them in the end.

For example, maybe your hero's Weakness is that he's the kind of guy who can't walk away from a crying woman, and that lands him in the middle of a messy domestic situation that turns tragic and gets him suspected of a murder he didn't commit. But his Strength is sharpshooting, and when the bad guy has the heroine on the top of a mountain, the hero can take him out at the critical moment.

In *Shrek*, Donkey's Weakness is his inability stop talking. That mouth is what gets him dumped in Shrek's swamp in the first place, and what gets the two of them in trouble with Lord Farquaad. Donkey's Strengths of loyalty and courage, however, save Shrek and Fiona from the dragon and also give him the right words to bring all of Shrek's friends together to rescue Fiona from the church.

Some Weaknesses are merely the other side of the coin of a Strength. A neat freak would also be obsessive about details, which in a job like accounting, would be a Strength. Think of Monk, the Character in the TV show by the same name. His OCD is a Weakness—but his obsessive attention to detail is a Strength. His OCD Weakness gets him in trouble over and over again (having to avoid certain situations, being late because he paused to straighten something out) and causes him to fail for the first forty-five minutes of the show. But his OCD also makes him remember details other investigators overlook and helps him catch the bad guy at the end.

Why does this work for a Plot? Because people are slow learners, and they need to have things increasingly spiral out of control before they "get it" and make changes in their lives (ask anyone on *Intervention* how true that is). The Increasing Stakes created by their Weaknesses force the Characters to face their Deepest fears (think of Shrek again, and the Scene in the church) and use their Strengths in order to get what they want most in the world.

We want active Characters, remember, and those Characters need to change and grow. We want to see them learn life lessons, become better people, and thus *deserve the happy ending we are creating for them*. Just as you must have a Plot arc where you go from Point A to Point B, you should also have an emotional arc for your Characters. That is where the Internal GMC comes into play and delivers emotional growth and change by the end of the book. In Shrek's emotional arc, he has learned to relate to people, be vulnerable, and open his heart. Donkey has learned to be more secure in himself and listen to others. Their Weaknesses aren't so weak at the end, because they have learned to rely on their Strengths (instead of acting out of fear or insecurity, which is often at the root of Weaknesses, but that's a Dr. Phil lesson for another day).

These two things—Increasing Stakes and the effective use of Weaknesses and Strengths—create stronger Conflicts in your book. They also create next-level Plots that have Twists and Turns and cliff-hangers that keep your reader up all night, dying to see how the next chapter ends.

Your Turn:

As you are working on your book, look at your Scenes and ask yourself: *How can my Character's Weakness get him into trouble here?* How can that cause the Plot to spiral in a new direction? Twist the actions to make them more compelling?

As you get to the ending Scenes of the book, ask yourself the opposite: *How can my Character's Strengths save the day?* How will that resolve the Plot? How will that show Character growth and change?

These two components of your Plot can turn it from blah to blockbuster. Maximize what you already have in your Character's makeup and in the powerful Plot you have created!

Scene Analysis

From *Their Unexpected Christmas Gift* by Shirley Jump

This is a longer scene analysis because I want to show you the progression from the beginning of the scene, through the middle, and into the end. Look for the scene goal, and the steps of the sequel. Also look for my analysis questions in all caps.

> By Wednesday, they had all settled into a routine. Vivian got up at five and was on the road to the office by six, long before Nick and Ellie woke up. She texted him every day before she left the office at six-thirty, and made any needed grocery runs on her way home. Meanwhile, Nick took care of Ellie, the house and made the meals. After dinner, more often than not, Vivian retreated to the dining room to work. If she got to bed before one in the morning, she considered it a good day. She knew she should help more with the household chores and Ellie, but Nick seemed to have it all under control, and she had a workload that seemed to grow by the minute. (WHAT IS SHE AVOIDING HERE WITH HER WORK? WHAT IS HER SCENE GOAL?)
>
> Several times throughout the day, she called and texted Sammie. She'd received one *I'm okay, don't worry*, but no other replies. Sammie had dropped

off the face of the earth. Vivian realized how little she knew about her sister—she had no idea where Sammie worked or who Sammie's friends were. Maybe she hadn't been as good of a sister as she'd thought. That troubled her, and nosed at the insecurities Vivian did her best to bury every day. (THESE INSECURITIES FORM THE BASIS OF HER DEEPEST CONFLICT IN THIS SCENE)

She pulled into the driveway of Nick's grandmother's house on Wednesday night, and realized she hadn't been outside during daylight hours in days. She left before the sun rose, returned after the sun had set. The only time she'd spent outside had been going to and from her car in the parking lot. Vivian turned off the sedan and glanced up at the house. (BACK TO AVOIDANCE HERE)

Two stories tall with a wide front porch, his late grandmother's home was painted a pale gray with lilac shutters and white trim. Rosebushes sat beneath the windows, with a thick lawn rolling toward the driveway and sidewalk. Far in the background sat Stone Gap Lake, a deep, dark blue oasis ringed by a few year-round homes.

But it was the golden light framed by the living room windows that drew her attention. Inside the house, she could see Nick, holding Ellie. He'd captured one of her little hands between two fingers and was smiling down at her.

As Vivian stepped out of the car, she heard music. A country song, Thomas Rhett, maybe, coming from inside the house. She stood in the driveway in the cold air, clutching the box of papers she needed to go through tonight, ignoring the weight of the overstuffed bag on her shoulder and the pain of her heels after a long day, and watched Nick glide around the room with her niece in his arms.

And felt like a failure. (WHAT DOES THIS MOMENT SHOW ABOUT VIVIAN AND HER DEEPEST EMOTIONAL FEARS?)

Nick made it look so easy. He had from the minute Ellie had dropped into his life. As far as she could tell, every time he picked Ellie up, she calmed down. Every time he changed her diaper, she looked up at him like he was the most adored human on the planet. And every time he held her, she placed her head on his chest and fisted his shirt in her palm, as if she never wanted to let go.

When Vivian picked up her niece, Ellie cried. When she changed Ellie's diaper, the baby squirmed and fussed and the tape went askew. When she held Ellie, her niece twisted away and pitched a fit.

Vivian glanced down at the box in her hands, the files and notes stuffed inside that needed to be looked over tonight. Maybe it was best if she just concentrated on her job. Jerry and his family were counting on her to make it right, to help them get back to normal lives. They needed her.

Ellie, clearly, did not. (WHAT IS VIVIAN MOST AFRAID OF HERE?)

Vivian turned, opened the rear door of her car and returned the box and her bag to the backseat. She dug out her keys and was about to open the driver's side door when Nick stepped onto the porch. He had Ellie wrapped in a blanket to keep out the cold. The country song floated in the air between them.

"Dinner's almost ready," he said.

"Actually…I'm not staying."

"You're leaving again already? Why? You just got here. If you want to hold Ellie for a minute—" he held her niece out to her, and as if on cue, Ellie began to scream and protest "—I can put the pasta in—"

"That's why I'm leaving, Nick. Because if I hold Ellie, she's going to scream. If I spend time with her, she's going to cry. And in the end, she's only going to want you anyway, so why should I even try?"

She shook her head before her damned emotions got ahold of her. Nick had drawn Ellie back to his chest, and in an instant, the infant went back to being happy and content. Even the thought of being with her aunt upset Ellie. How could Vivian be any kind of parent to a kid who hated the sight of her? Nick was a thousand times better at this than she was. "I have a lot of work to do tonight—"

"You've had a lot of work to do every night, Vivian. And every morning. And all day."

"It's my job, Nick. That's what they pay me to do." It occurred to her that they sounded like a bickering married couple. When had that happened? When had they gone from strangers to friends to some sort of weird partners?

"Not to the exclusion of having a life, Vivian. If you ask me, you're just using the work as an excuse to avoid living. Your sister clearly isn't the only one who runs away." He turned on his heel and went back into the house. (NICK CALLS HER OUT ON HER FEARS)

Vivian stood there, fuming in the cold. How dare he tell her how to live her life? To imply she was missing out by being a workaholic? Or that she was running away? Okay, so maybe some of that was true, but as soon as this lawsuit was over…

She shut the car door, marched up the stairs and into the house, ready to tell Nick off. She stopped in the middle of the hallway. In the last few days, she'd come home, beelined to the kitchen for a quick bite to eat, then rushed to the dining room for a couple hours of work, then took the back staircase up to her room in the wee hours of the morning. She hadn't had a moment to pause and look at the rest of the house.

The living room she had been in on Monday, with the couch that was as comfortable as a slice of heaven, was in the process of being transformed. Evergreen garlands wove in and out of fat white pillar candles on the fireplace mantel, and beneath that, a fire burned, safely behind a wrought-iron grate she didn't remember seeing before. A ceramic miniature Christmas tree with hundreds of tiny lights sat on the end table, and the plain glass bowl on the coffee table was now overflowing with red ribbons and thick pine cones. A pillow-sized fat stuffed Santa sat on the sofa, against a thick afghan printed with a snowy mountain scene. The hallway rug beneath her feet had been switched out for a white-and-blue one imprinted with a holiday scene of children sledding down the long runner.

The words she'd planned to fling at Nick died in her throat. "When did you do all this?"

"Over the last couple of days. Whenever Ellie was napping, I'd go up to my grandmother's attic and unearth some more boxes. I had…something I was supposed to find up there, but then I came across the Christmas decorations and figured it would be nice to put them up. So Ellie and I decorated."

Something he was supposed to find in his grandmother's attic? He didn't elaborate and she didn't ask. She did notice a lone box tucked away in the corner that was marked *Nick*, but didn't question it. This whole thing was temporary, a blip in her life, and getting more personal would be a mistake. "Ellie and you decorated?"

"Yep. I made her do all the heavy lifting while I watched." He grinned at the baby in his arms. "She's got quite the eye for mantel design."

"The room looks beautiful." She stowed her purse and keys on the end table, then stepped into the living room and did a slow spin. "It already looks like Christmas."

"Well, it will. We still need a tree. A real tree, not some plastic fake one that never sheds a needle." He waved toward the corner of the room. A few days ago, a small armchair had sat there. Now, the armchair had been moved to flank the sofa, leaving a blank space between the far left front windows and the wall. A stack of boxes labeled *Ornaments* was sitting on the floor beside the space. "I know this is a temporary situation with the three of us here, but I figured since it was Ellie's first Christmas, she might like the lights and stuff. She already thinks that Santa on the couch is a toy just for her."

Hard-nosed, dedicated, driven Vivian found herself tearing up for the third time in one week. Who was this man? And how did he happen to come into her life—and Ellie's life—exactly when they needed someone like him?

"So why don't you stay here tonight," Nick said, taking Vivian's hand and leading her farther into the living room, "and not work, and spend time with your niece and the man who made you fettuccini Alfredo for dinner?"

His hand felt nice on hers. Warm, safe, dependable. She curled her fingers over his. "You made fettuccini Alfredo? That's my favorite."

"I know. You mentioned it a couple days ago."

"And you remembered?" Damn it. Now her throat was thick, and her heart was full of some emotion she didn't recognize. She'd dated several men over the years, got sort of serious with a couple of them, but not a one could have named her favorite food, the flowers she loved best, or how she took her coffee in the morning. Nick paid attention to details—maybe that was part of the chef in him— and she'd already seen it pay dividends in the way he seemed to have an intuitive sense of what made Ellie happy.

And apparently, he also had a sense of what made Vivian choke up.

"Don't work tonight, Vivian," he said again, softer this time. "Let's eat and then go buy a tree and decorate it tonight. I bet Ellie will love the lights."

She thought of the box in her car. Jerry sitting in the office conference room a few months ago and begging her to help them. The hours she and her team had put into this lawsuit already. She'd unearthed almost enough evidence of shoddy workmanship on the part of the manufacturer that she could go to them and hopefully negotiate a settlement and avoid a drawn-out lawsuit for that man and his family. Almost enough. A couple more days of work, and hopefully she'd have a solid argument for a hefty settlement.

"I have people depending on me," she said.

"You have a niece depending on you, too."

Vivian looked over at Nick. Ellie was nestled against his shoulder, her wide blue eyes fixed on his shirt. Her fist opened and closed over the soft cotton. "No, Nick. She's depending on you. And if you ask me, that's her best bet. Because I'm a lousy mother. And sister."

And I'm bailing just like Sammie did, bailing on Ellie, bailing on whatever this thing with Nick is.

Then she headed out of the house, got back in her car and drove to her apartment in Durham. At least there she wouldn't feel guilty staying up all night working and catching a nap on the futon in the spare room. And she wouldn't have to be reminded every time she turned around that she was letting down the one person she had sworn she'd never disappoint. (IN THIS SCENE, DID SHE GET HER SCENE GOAL (OF WORKING TO AVOID EVERYTHING)? AND WHAT PRICE DID SHE PAY FOR THAT? HOW DID THAT IMPACT HER DEEPEST EMOTIONAL FEARS?)

PART THREE
COMPELLING CHARACTERS

CHAPTER SEVEN
FIRST, YOU HAVE TO GIVE A DAMN

You can have an amazing Plot, some really great Scenes, and your book can still feel flat because compelling books also have one more key ingredient: compelling Characters.

We've already talked about the key components of compelling Scenes. But even the best written Scene will fall flat if the Characters aren't amazing and compelling themselves. When we put down a book we loved—or even better, recommend it to a friend—ninety-nine percent of the time it was the Characters we loved and related to, far more than the Plot.

What makes for a compelling Character? Look at the books you read, the shows you watch. Which Characters draw you in the most? Which ones have you hooked and coming back time and again? Analyze everything from comedies to dramas, from sitcoms to movies. As I write this, I'm watching *Friends* for the seven millionth time. I think I've seen every episode at least a dozen times. I love the Characters—they're relatable and vulnerable and most of all, compelling. I know what happens when Monica runs into Richard at the same time Chandler is planning on proposing, yet I keep watching because the Characters are almost friends to me, too. That's the best part about compelling Characters—your reader will imagine them as part of their life, too.

Take an especially close look at the "unusual" Characters who hook you. Hannibal Lecter from *Silence of the Lambs*. Jax from *Sons of Anarchy*. Reacher from the Lee Child novels. Sayid from *Lost*. These are the Characters who, on paper, wouldn't seem compelling. An Iraqi torturer? An intelligent cannibal? A violent gang member? Yet they are compelling and memorable, both in books and movies.

They Are a Cut Above the Rest

Compelling Characters are ones who don't fit the norm. They are people who make questionable decisions yet still manage to resonate with readers and viewers (like the man who pretends to be Jack Sommersby in Sommersby). They are multi-dimensional Characters who often have dark sides that are tempered by strong moral compasses, flickers of conscience, and/or incredibly interesting personas (like Hannibal Lecter).

Take Jax from *Sons of Anarchy*, the show about a motorcycle gang in California. This is a classic good versus evil show—the "good" Feds and cops against the "bad" motorcycle gang who is trafficking in guns.

No doubt about it, the SOA gang does some very bad things. They kill people. They torture people. They run a business producing hard core porn videos. They sometimes even kill their own. They have an interesting job that is far outside the realm of the rest of us, and when you watch the show, you are part of their world. And at the same time, you can't tear yourself away, no matter how hard you try because that dark side, mixed with a strong moral code, creates a gripping show that hooks you early and keeps you hooked.

They Love, and Love Deeply

The one thing that Jax (and all the others) have is an unbreakable devotion to family, both their blood family and their gang family. There is nothing they wouldn't do to protect those they love, and no stone they'd leave unturned if one of their own is missing. You see quiet moments where Jax is holding his baby or talking to his mother, and you see a multi-dimensional man who is basically just trying to do the right thing. Granted, their version of right and wrong is a little skewed from the rest of the world's, but it's close enough that you can relate to their care and concern.

When Jax's infant son is kidnapped, the viewer already knows that he will do whatever it takes to get his child back. He does step over the line of the law many times, but as a viewer, you can see his pain and desperation and you can relate. You find yourself cheering for him, even when he does something you might not support in any other circumstance.

They Are Relatable

Relatability is a major part of creating a compelling Character. You can make them do the most heinous or generous things, if their actions are properly motivated. With proper Motivation, a Character can commit a crime, kill someone, or give away their kidney, and the reader will be captivated because they can empathize or even put themselves in that Character's shoes. Even Tony Soprano, the famed fictional mob boss, has his moments where what he is doing is undoubtedly wrong and almost evil, but you understand because he is protecting his family. In the end, that's what Tony does everything for—his family.

You need to find the elements of your Character that everyone can relate to. There are commonalities among everyone—love of family, love of children, fear of failure, etc. Reacher, from the Lee Child novels, is a loner with a checkered past in the Army. He crosses the line sometimes, but that's because he is living his life by his rules; rules based firmly on wrong and right. He does what he must to protect and save the weaker among us. You can relate to him, care about him, and support his actions because in the end, he's doing the right thing, and that's something many of us can understand.

On *Lost*, Sayid, an Iraqi Republican Guard soldier who tortured people before he landed on the island, had perhaps one of the most reprehensible careers among the cast. But as the show wore on, you learned how what he had to do tortured Sayid as much as those he hurt. He paid a huge price for his career and decided long ago that he would do whatever it took to protect and save his friends. Sayid is a loyal and generous man, the kind you want behind or beside you when things get dicey.

They Are Strong

Compelling Characters are can-do Characters. They have moments of doubt—everyone does—but they don't stand there waffling for twenty minutes. They make a decision, good or bad, and they stick with it. Reacher, for instance, runs through a quick paragraph or two of the pros and cons of his decisions, and in the end, usually chooses the one with fewer cons because it's the right decision, the one that protects or saves the most people. He is prepared to make sacrifices, even get hurt himself, as long as the outcome is the right one.

These are Characters you can depend on in a crisis. They can be affable and funny (think of Mike Rowe on *Dirty Jobs*,) or stern and almost scary (think of Dirty Harry) but in the end, if you had to pick one person in the room to have with you on an adventure, that's the name that comes to mind. Their spirits don't break easily and even when everything seems lost, they forge forward. Because that's all they know how to do.

Compelling Characters don't sit and wallow. They <u>act</u>.

The Scenes Bring Out the Best in Them

Every interaction that the Character has in a Scene should bring out a little more of his or her Backstory. *Lost* does this exceptionally well, by dropping in little bits of Backstory into each episode. We'll talk more about Backstory in a future chapter, but the basic concept of Backstory is that it is used at key moments (meaning when the Character would naturally think about their history) to add emotion and depth to a Scene.

No matter what your Character is doing, the Scene should Show (not Tell) what kind of person your Character is. Are they nice? Angry? Impatient? Kind to kittens? Are they worried about losing their job? Protective of their best friend? Whatever happens in the Scene, whatever road your Character follows, should Show them in the best possible light—even if they are the villain. Show the villain at his most villainous, or Show him as multi-dimensional with a tender moment. Let the Scene do the work of bringing out a new dimension of your Character.

Change is what fosters growth and growth is what creates compelling Characters.

In addition, the Scenes need to keep the reader's attention and move the Plot forward. You should never have a Scene where nothing happens. No one wants to watch—or read about—someone sitting on their sofa for hours. The Plot needs to keep moving along, with every single Scene. What does that mean for your Character? It means things are constantly changing in their world.

Give Them a Difficult Choice

Compelling Characters are often stuck in no-win situations. Think of all the movies and books you have loved, where the Character is often stuck having to make an impossible choice. Does she sacrifice herself to save her son? Does he give up the dream job so that he can restore his family? Does he kill his mother to protect his child?

Remember the chapter on Motivation? You can make any difficult choice work if the Character has a strong enough Motivation. That whole thing about killing your own mother? Go watch the last season of *Sons of Anarchy* and see Jax wrestle with that very principle because his mother has become toxic and dangerous for his family. It's the kind of choice that has viewers on the edges of their seats—or readers turning the pages like crazy.

It doesn't have to be a life-or-death choice. Great sitcoms and comedies are written about tough choices, too. Take a light movie like *Paul Blart: Mall Cop* or *When Harry Met Sally.* Those Characters have choices to make, choices that will dramatically impact their lives and the lives of people they care about. The reason why those choices and stories work is because the Characters are compelling.

Good, strong Characters are about good writing. Characters who come alive *have* lives, pasts, Goals, wishes, dreams, hurts, and foibles. You can see, touch, feel, and hear their lives when you read the words on the page. That's what draws the reader in, keeps them up late at night, and makes them recommend your book—and auto-buy your next one!

Give Them a Layered Past

People who have had flat, uninteresting pasts don't make for interesting people in the present. The guy who grew up with two parents and lived in the same house all his life and had a puppy that became his best friend…blah, blah…that guy doesn't become a Jax or Sayid or Reacher (it's the same with other gendered Characters). Batman became Batman because of what happened to his parents. Not because he was wealthy or privileged or went to the opera a lot.

Compelling Characters need to be heroic and to have something worth fighting for, whether that's saving the family home or saving the world. Will Smith's Character in *Seven Pounds* makes some questionable choices, but in the end, you see why, and you understand. The last choice he has to make is a heartbreaker. No matter which way he goes, someone will lose, and you feel his pain as he fills that tub.

They need to have worthy Adversaries, too. It's no fun to have a great, strong hero, and pit him against a wimpy Villain who crumples at the first sign of trouble. Your Character needs to be battling someone who is as strong as they are. Whether it's the birth mother trying to get her child back (*Losing Isaiah*) or the wizard who feels he was wrongly convicted (*Harry Potter*), you should give your compelling Character an equally compelling Antagonist.

Your Turn:

Look at your main Character and think about what he/she is fighting for. Is it something that is vitally important? Something they will risk their lives to attain? Will this goal require making a difficult choice or a sacrifice?

Scene Analysis

This snippet from David Joy's book, *When These Mountains Burn*[4], shows the complicated layers of the father/son relationship in just a few paragraphs. You can see the house, the relationship he had with his wife, and the history with his son, along with the anger and yet love that still exists. I love David Joy as an author, by the way. He is a master of compelling storytelling. Look at the details that Joy uses to show Ray's character.

---

4   David Joy, *When These Mountains Burn* (New York, G.P. Putnam & Sons, 2020), 272.

He was almost finished with his glass when the phone rang inside the house. A cane-back rocker was nestled in the corner of the front room where his wife used to sit and talk with her sister and her friends and telemarketers and anyone else who'd listen because truth was that woman just loved to talk. Her and Ray had balanced each other out that way, him never saying boo to a goose and her having enough stowed away for the both of them.

"Talk to me," Ray grumbled into the receiver. His voice was deep and gruff, words never seeming to make it out of the back of his throat. The stub of his cigar was hooked in the corner of his mouth and he scissored the butt between two fingers so as to clear his lips to speak. He could hear heavy breathing on the other end of the line, but no one said a word. "Hello."

"Dad," a voice whimpered, "Dad ..." He was out of breath. "They're going to kill me."

Raymond ran his hand down his face and stretched his eyes, trying to will his wits about him. He started to hang up, but hesitated. His hand clenched the phone so hard that he could hear the plastic cracking in his fist.

The boy's voice was the same as when he'd been ten years old and called from Gary Green's, having burned down the man's barn with a G.I. Joe, a magnifying glass, and a Dixie cup of kerosene. It was the same as the first time Ricky got arrested, and the second and the third, the same scared-to-death, I'm-in-over-my-head horseshit Ray'd heard so many times over the course of his life that he couldn't bear to listen. He was almost immune. Yet, right then, same as always, he found himself incapable of hanging up.

.

CHAPTER EIGHT

CIRCLING BACK TO THE WORST NIGHTMARE

We talked about the Worst Nightmare back in the chapter on Plot, but now we're going to tie it in with Characters a little bit more. Remember, when you force your Characters to face their Worst Nightmares, they are also *forced to face their Deepest Emotional Fears*. Ooh, it just got real in here. Grab some Kleenexes.

So...What Is Their Deepest Emotional Fear?

Deepest Emotional Fears come from the emotional scars your Characters have. You know, the kind of stuff that people go on Dr. Phil and talk about. Abuse, abandonment, insecurity, addiction, rejection...there's a long list of things that we can be terrified of. A child whose mother left her on a doorstep when she was one may grow up to be an adult who can't commit to anyone—or someone who gets super clingy. A child who was physically abused may be the kind that is terrified of confrontation, or a perfectionist, or desperate to please others.

Basically, what screwed your Character up when he/she was a child? How did that event change the way they handle stress, the way they react to conflict, the types of relationships they have? What situations does your Character do their best to avoid? Where is their comfort zone? And what is the worst possible thing that could happen, and thus yank them out of that comfort zone?

When you work on these answers, I want you to go deeper than surface replies. For example, how does your Character cope with stressful situations? If the answer is "she eats ice cream," that's not an answer that's going to help you a whole lot in Plotting. It's not going to get you even remotely close to the Worst Nightmare scenario (even if you create a worldwide ice cream shortage!).

The Character who eats ice cream when she is stressed is probably doing that for more than a sugar craving. Maybe she gets scared when she has a lot of pressure and falls back into addictive patterns. Maybe she isolates herself from her loved ones. Maybe she avoids the tasks or decisions she has to make. These are the kind of inner issues that feed into a Worst Nightmare. So ask the questions, but dig deeper on the answers.

Try Asking Why

If you are having trouble digging deep, then simply ask *Why*. Why does my heroine go straight for the Rocky Road when she's having a bad day? Why does my hero avoid being alone? Why does my heroine always say yes when she wants to say no?

Asking Why is your best way, hands-down, of learning who your Character is deep down inside. We all have a Why for everything we do. I shop when I'm stressed (hey, don't judge me by my Amazon order history!). Partly because retail therapy is a thing, but more so because shopping allows me to procrastinate (I'm a master time waster when I'm trying to find the perfect dress).

And why do I do this? What am I avoiding by shopping? All those things that are stressing me out, like deadlines. Except... procrastinating only compounds the problem, so the stress increases when I get home with my overburdened credit card and a lot of shopping bags. It's a self-defeating behavior, and if I were putting myself in a book, I would use that self-sabotage as a Plot tool. I would create a scenario where that self-defeating behavior ruins my Character's life. Sound like a familiar Plot? It is—in the bestselling *Confessions of a Shopaholic* by Sophie Kinsella.

There's Power in Failure

Failure has taught me more than success ever has—true story. I have failed a thousand times more than I have succeeded, but I'm grateful for all those failures because they have taught me many things—I am stronger than I knew, I can keep going even when I want to quit, and a hard-earned success is so much sweeter than an easy win.

Your Characters need to fail, fail, fail, and then finally triumph.

In the process, they will grow and change, and your reader will bond with them even more. There's a reason everyone roots for the underdog. Their determination and tireless can-do spirit is super inspiring. It shows the rest of us that we can eventually conquer our fears and setbacks, too. Characters who fail over and over again and then succeed are the kind of Characters who are endearing and memorable. They're people we relate to, root for, and say, *hey, I can be them when I grow up!*

Look at the movie *Runaway Bride,* for example. In that movie, Julia Roberts' Character tries and fails over and over again to marry her Mister Right. Why? Because her Deepest Emotional Fear—her Worst Nightmare—is being lost in a relationship. Of having to subdue who she really is for someone else. Yet what does she do over and over again? Contort and twist herself to fit her current man's picture of his perfect woman. It's not until Julia figures out who she truly is on her own, without a man to define her, that she can be ready for and find happiness. That Scene in the diner with the eggs, where she realizes she has no idea what kind of eggs she likes because she's been ordering the dishes that her boyfriends liked, is a key turning point for her Character. It's what eventually spurs her to FedEx her way out of her wedding to Richard Gere. Deep down inside, she knows she hasn't quite found herself and thus, isn't ready for marriage to anyone.

Stephen King has built a career out of people's Worst Nightmares (clowns, anyone?). But at their core, his books are about much more than just rabid dogs and reincarnated pets. They are about people who must face the thing they are most afraid of, whether it's being responsible for a little brother who goes missing to facing the reality that we all eventually die. You can do the same thing, regardless of what genre you write.

The Worst Nightmare is a great Plot tool because it creates a situation where the stakes will get worse (as they should) because your Character is having to face their Deepest Emotional Fears.

Okay, You've Sold Me, Now What?

How do you figure out your Character's Worst Nightmare? You go back to those questions you asked yourself a second ago. You pile those answers up next to any other Character development and Plot planning you have done. Then you ask yourself one big question:

What is the worst possible thing that can happen to this person?

I don't mean a catastrophe (like losing a limb) necessarily. I mean the thing that will upset their perfect little apple-cart world. The thing that jolts them out of their comfort zone and into a world they would rather avoid entirely. Rick Grimes, in the first episode of *The Walking Dead,* wakes up to his Worst Nightmare—losing his family. Technically, he has already lost them because his marriage is in trouble before the series even starts. He not only has to battle zombies, wander all over Georgia searching for them, and deal with some hairy life-and-death moments, but once he's reunited with Lori and Carl, he needs to do some emotional rebuilding, too. By the time Rick reaches them and truly reunites, you are rooting so hard for him to make it work. *The Walking Dead* is brilliant because it starts where the trouble starts—and the trouble is not the zombies. They are just a Conflict in Rick's way.

You've all probably heard that sage Plot advice to start where the trouble starts. Writers tell me all the time—that's great, but how do I know what the trouble is?

Answer: it's the Worst Nightmare (see how easy I just made that?). The "trouble" is the one thing your Character doesn't want to have happen and it stems from those Deep Emotional Fears and Issues.

As we talked about before, Shrek's Worst Nightmare is to be around people and thus, to be rejected, hurt, or vilified. What trouble starts the story off? Fairy tale creatures get dumped in his swamp, and those unwelcome guests are compounded by Donkey, who won't leave, no matter what, and then compounded again by the task of having to go get Princess Fiona. People make fun of him, they come after him with pitchforks, they laugh at him. Everywhere Shrek turns, he is facing his Worst Nightmare. You feel sorry for him because you can relate to the pain he is going through. And in the end, when all that dealing with his issues makes him grow and change and take a risk on love, you are cheering him on and rooting for him to win Fiona over.

That's what the Worst Nightmare accomplishes—it creates Characters we can bond with and root for. We cheer the endings, cry because they succeeded, and then rush to recommend or buy the next book. The Worst Nightmare very often leads to the happiest of endings!

Your Turn:

1. Pick any movie, book, sitcom, etc., and choose one Character to analyze. Why is that Character compelling? What draws you back time and time again to watch the show or read the book? Next, take your own work, and give your main Character one more element to make them more compelling. Maybe you choose a tortured past memory or a difficult choice or moment of strength. Whatever layer you add to this Character, be sure to make it one that creates an emotional bond with the reader.

2. If you're having trouble figuring this out for your own Characters, then do this. Pick three movies or books and pinpoint the main Character's Worst

Nightmare. Remember, it should stem from their Deep Emotional Fears. Then figure out how the director/author used that to create a fantastic Plot based on the Character facing their fears.

From there, go back to your WIP Character. Use their unhealthy coping mechanisms, Internal issues, and the things they avoid most in the world, and create the Worst Nightmare from there. What's the Worst Nightmare for a perfectionist? Chaos. What's the Worst Nightmare for a public figure? Humiliation. What's the Worst Nightmare for a wealthy playboy? Poverty.

After that, ask yourself one more question about your Character. Why is this my Character's Worst Nightmare? What deep Emotional Fears arise if this happens? And how can I use this to make my Character fail, over and over again, and earn a happy ending?

Scene Analysis

This excerpt is from *The Well*, a young adult horror novel I wrote with my daughter under the pen name A.J. Whitten. In this scene, Cooper is torn between wanting to trust his mother and being afraid that is working for the creature that is trying to kill him. His Worst Nightmare is finding out the mother he loves so much is behind all the horror that has been happening in town—in other words, realizing the world he thought he knew doesn't exist.

I made it as far as the washing machine.

She found me in the basement next to the Maytag, standing in my underwear, with the dirty clothes in one hand, the other hand reaching for the metal lid. "Cooper. What are you doing?"

I froze. Cursed. Goose bumps danced up my spine and my guts twisted like a pretzel. It wasn't just that I was a teenage boy caught doing laundry. In an ordinary home, that would be suspicious. Ordinary mothers would suspect stealing, snorting coke, hosting orgies in the afternoon or something equally illegal or weird, like the world suddenly coming to an end. But this wasn't an ordinary house and she was no ordinary mother. I had to grip the edge of the washer before I could force a word past my lips. "Nothing."

She reached past me, and I could smell her perfume, the one she'd worn for as long as I could remember. Something that reminded me of fruit. I forgot the name of it, but it came in a red box and cost like sixty bucks. I remember because my stepfather had bought some last Christmas and groaned about how he could have gotten a chainsaw or a leafblower for that amount of money. Even though he could well afford two hundred boxes of the stuff. My stepfather came from generations of wealth, worked two days a week as an OB/GYN, owned a vineyard that practically poured money into his pockets, yet was as tight with his money as a lunch lady with seconds on pizza day. In the year and a half they'd been married, I'd never understood what my mother had seen in him, other than maybe a checkbook. Faulkner and I worked on staying out of his way and counting down the days until we turned eighteen.

My mother's arm brushed against my shoulder. Her perfume no longer smelled like her, or like my childhood.

It smelled like fear.

Everything inside me turned to ice. Another part didn't want to believe it. That stupid part that kept believing in accidents and chalking the whole thing up to one intense case of PMS.

"Cooper, you can't do that."

I waited. Waited for her to grab me again, yank me out of there with some excuse about looking for the dog, lying to me about him being lost, and then when we got near the well, she'd grab me again by the back of the neck and drag me to the edge, and before I could think, react, dig in my heels, stop her, she would throw me down, down into that deep dark hole.

And this time, this time, I wouldn't get out.

DOWNLOAD MY FREE HANDOUT

"The Highlighter Method of Learning to Plot" at JumpStartCreativeSolutions.com

CHAPTER NINE
I HAVE A POINT HERE, I PROMISE

And my point is…Point of View is important. And that, kids, is why I don't have a career in comedy.

In all seriousness, Point of View is one of the most impactful tools in your writing arsenal. It's also one of those things that is tough for beginning writers, but once you understand the concept, it can be easy to master.

Using POV in a book is about much more than choosing which Character will tell the story. Used effectively, POV can amp up the emotion, strengthen the Plot, and make your book compelling and unforgettable. A strong POV creates a book that leaves readers crying and wanting more because they have bonded so tightly with the Characters that the fictional people seem like friends.

The Cocktail Party Curse of Head-Hopping

Why is POV important? Because it *builds a relationship* between the reader and the Character. It forms nodes of connection that make the reader care and engage. That's why head-hopping is such a no-no in books.

Think of it this way: Imagine going to a cocktail party with a dozen people you are just meeting for the first time. The hostess Jane opens the door and starts to tell you about her mysterious past in New York, but just as you get intrigued, nosy Nancy introduces herself and begins talking about her orchids. Then chatty Charles steps in to introduce himself and talk about his suspicions about the town's mayor, just as Jane comes back and starts talking again. You're meeting person after person, and not having any time to build that connection with any single person, and before you know it, the party is a blur of faces and stories. It's like speed dating Characters.

> Point of View builds a relationship between the reader and the Character. Use it to create the strongest emotional impact.

That's what head-hopping (switching POVs several times within a Scene) does. It weakens the relationship the reader has with the Characters. Some authors, like Nora Roberts, can head hop seamlessly, but it's not as easy as she makes it look. Your best bet is to give each major Character a few Scenes in just their POV so the reader connects with and knows them before you start switching POV within a Scene. That way, the reader is intrigued, as you were with Jane's New York City secrets, and has bonded enough with the Character to want to see how things turn out. In a best-case scenario, the author creates such strong bonds with both Antagonists and Protagonists that the reader wants both Characters to win. Which equals…Conflict on the page just because of the emotional ties.

Pluses and Minuses of Different Types of POV

When using POV, the first decision you have to make is which type to use. Sometimes, I try an opening Scene in one type of POV, then the other, to see which feels more like the Character. There are several basic types of POV:

Omniscient: This is when one narrator tells the story from a remote viewpoint, usually in the third person. Omniscient refers to it being a "god-like" perspective of the narrator seeing from afar. The Omniscient POV knows all, including what each of the Characters are thinking and feeling, but that also creates some distance in the relationship with the reader because it never delivers a really close look inside one Character's head. It's like the difference between a synopsis and a deep dive analysis of a story.

First Person: This is a book written from the narrator's perspective, using "I" for the POV. *The Great Gatsby*, for instance, uses first person, where there is a single narrator who tells the story from his perspective. The biggest drawback to this POV is that the reader can only see what the narrator can see. They can't see the history of the neighbor down the street, can't witness the murder in the house behind them. They can't know what others are thinking unless they tell them. If you choose to write in first person, make sure you stay only in that person's viewpoint, and don't add things to their thoughts that it would be impossible for them to know or intuit. Think about the writing as the way you see things and your world— you can guess at what your partner is thinking but you don't really know.

First Person POV can also be problematic if your narrator isn't likeable. The audience needs to latch on to this person and care about them relatively early in the story. An unlikeable narrator makes it tough to create that connection. If the connection isn't there, the reader will put the book down and never pick it up again.

As a general rule, regardless of which type of POV you choose, make sure the story is *told from the viewpoint of the person who has the most to lose or the most changes to make* (more on this in a minute). Gatsby would have been an entirely different book if told from Daisy's POV or from Gatsby's. Nick, really, had the most to change and the most to lose in some ways, so his perspective made sense. *White Oleander* does first person well and is a great example of using the POV of a Character who loses and learns the most.

Second Person: This POV is rarely, if ever used. This "you" Point of View is far too confusing. McInerney's *Bright Lights,*

Big City[5] is one of the more well-known examples of Second Person POV. It's a tough one to write well and makes it very difficult to build that relationship between the reader and the Character because the "you" creates a sense of distance. Here's a snippet from Jay McInerney's book: *'Things happen, people change,' is what Amanda said. For her that covered it. You wanted an explanation, and ending that would assign blame and dish up justice. You considered violence and you considered reconciliation. But what you are left with is a premonition of the way your life will fade behind you, like a book you have read too quickly, leaving a dwindling trail of images and emotions, until all you can remember is a name.*

Third Person: Third Person POV, the most common type, chooses certain Characters to be the voice of the story. The deeper you can go with Third Person POV, the closer the reader gets to your Character. It allows the author to show what's in the Character's heart and soul, which helps readers to latch on and become more deeply invested in the Character's plight.

The most effective type of Third Person POV is Deep Third Person POV, because it goes even further getting into the Character's head. If you can interchange the word "I" with the pronoun for your third person Character, then you're very likely writing in Deep Third Person POV. Deep POV always maintains a clear delineation between Characters (men vs.

---

5   Jay McInerney, *Bright Lights, Big City* (New York, Vintage Books, 1984), 182.

women, old vs. young, Southern vs. Northern) in the inner monologue. It sounds as if you are talking to that person, because their thoughts are as powerful as the dialogue. The Character's past, present, and environment affect their manner of speaking and their reactions. In Deep Third Person POV, that layering is even more evident.

No matter which viewpoint you choose to write in, when using POV, keep these tips in mind:

1. **Don't Make it Weird**: Just as you wouldn't insert extra information you already knew in your own thoughts, don't do it when you are in a Character's POV. It's that stereotypical soap opera recap: "the brother she had that her father had disowned when he married his third wife". Throwing all this information comes off as an info dump. If the information is necessary to the Plot, work it into the story in another way, such as through conversation or other Characters' dialogue.

2. **A Character can only see what is past their eyes.** Meaning, they don't see their hair color or eye color, or even think about it. How many of us think about our appearance if we aren't in front of a mirror? It's very rare and should be for your Characters, too. A Character who thinks about her "lovely flowing brown locks" sounds shallow, self-centered, and conceited.

3. **Choosing which POV to put a Scene in matters.** It might not seem like it does, but it does matter, a lot.

You want to choose the Character with the **most to lose** or the **most to learn**. That automatically ups the emotional stakes. And that's really, in the end, what you want to do—create drama, emotion, and Tension.

4. **The number one thing most people forget is to filter everything that POV Character sees through his/her past, present, and prejudices.** A Texas cowboy will see things differently than a Manhattan socialite. A Texas cowboy who was beaten repeatedly as a child will see things differently than a cowboy brought up privileged and happy. A socialite with a devastating past will see things differently than one who has spent her life in a glass world. A claustrophobic will look at a closet differently than a child looking for a hiding place.

5. **Speaking of pasts, don't forget to use that in every Scene.** We are all shaped by our past histories. Someone who has been raped will be afraid of dark areas, but also afraid of being alone and afraid of trusting others. Someone who was beaten will be hyper-sensitive to abuse against others. Someone who was brought up in an alcoholic home will have that experience color everything they do. Their pasts create their Deepest Emotional Fears, their Weaknesses, and their Strengths, and you need to keep that in mind in every single Scene. Those emotional impacts from their histories color their thoughts, perceptions, and dialogue.

For example: In Cinderella, Cinderella was brought up by a kind father, and that has turned her into someone who is kind to those less fortunate. She is hardened, however, by the experiences of living with her cruel stepmother and has learned not to expect anything for herself. Her stepsisters, on the other hand, have known nothing but the cruel tongue and hand of their mother, and they are in turn cruel to Cinderella. In addition, the stepsisters have developed an almost Darwinian survival of the fittest approach because they have witnessed how quickly their mother can turn on them. So their cruelty isn't just a Character flaw, it's a protection against becoming the next Cinderella of the family. And Cinderella, rather than striving to be in the favored position her stepsisters have, has learned to trust and bond with the lowliest of creatures because their hearts are open, and their motives are true.

So, think back on the movie/book—how do those pasts for each of the daughters in Cinderella color their actions, reactions, and dialogue? How do they view themselves? The world around them? The challenges that come up in the story?

6. **Study great POV to write great POV.** Too often, we are rushing through the action and forget to take a moment to allow the narrative to unfold and the Character reactions to add depth and Tension. Study

books that linger in your heart and mind. Chances are, the writer has used POV to its utmost. I was watching an overview of *Schitt's Creek* yesterday and one of the things a reporter said made the show fabulous was that the writers didn't just write great dialogue, they allowed room for the emotions and *impact* of those moments to show. You should do that in your work, too.

7. **POV should show in every element of that Character's Scene**—in the Character's inner thoughts, in the way they dress, in the way they speak. Our past, present, and perceptions are reflected in our manner of speaking, the way we treat others, the choices we make in everything from soap to shoes. Think of the Texas cowboy vs. the socialite—how will their experiences and perceptions affect every detail of their Character? The way they talk? Now take the cowboy who was abused and is slow to trust—how will he show that wall in his attitude, his demeanor, his clothes, his walk, his talk?

This is a vital point, folks—you want the POV Characters to not just perceive the world through the filter of their past/present and perceptions, but to *show* those things in their actions. That creates true depth of Character on the page and takes POV to a stronger, more compelling level.

Your Turn:

Choose a Setting, say, a busy intersection at night, and then write three paragraphs in different POVs of a variety of Characters, like a child, an elderly woman, a cowboy, or a car thief. What will they notice? What will scare them? What will their eyes be drawn to? What reactions will they have to the traffic, the darkness, the time of day?

Scene Analysis

To write good POV, you have to read and study good POV. Some authors simply make me want to try harder as a writer, like Joshilyn Jackson and her awesome first-person opening to *Gods in Alabama*[6]:

> There are gods in Alabama: Jack Daniel's, high school quarterbacks, trucks, big tits, and also Jesus. I left one back there myself, back in Possett. I kicked it under the kudzu and left it to the roaches.
>
> I made a deal with God two years before I left there. At the time, I thought He made out pretty well. I

---

6   Joshilyn Jackson, *Gods in Alabama* (New York, Warner Books, 2006), 306.

offered Him a three-for-one-deal: All He had to do was perform a miracle. He fulfilled His end of the bargain, so I kept my three promises faithfully, no matter what the cost. I held our deal as sacred for twelve solid years. But that was before God let Rose Mae Lolley show up on my doorstep, dragging my ghosts and her own considerable baggage with her.

Go back and study those two paragraphs. What do you know about the character before you even meet her? What's important to her? What is she afraid of? What makes her likeable already?

The deeper you go into Character development, the stronger your POVs will be. You eventually get to a point where you learn to filter every part of the Scene through that Character's lens, and that's when you create Characters that people connect with and love!

PART FOUR
COMPELLING WRITING

CHAPTER TEN
DON'T GO SLOW IN THE FAST LANE

Here's a secret: if you want to make your reader stop reading, close your book, and let it gather dust on the shelf, put in a lot of Backstory. If you don't want any of those things to happen, then pay attention to this chapter because having a deft hand with Backstory can make the pacing of your book more powerful and keep your reader up until two in the morning, desperate to find out how things end.

The problem with Backstory is that writers feel compelled to tell everything they can in the beginning of the book. They're so sure the reader will get confused if they don't know the Characters' entire life stories. *But my reader needs to know this, so they understand the Character.*

Nope. They don't. They need to be *intrigued* by your Character. If they are intrigued, they will want to read more, and they will hold on for the ride so they can uncover the pieces of your Character's past that have gone into making them so interesting.

For a year or so, I did online dating (and yes, it was as awful as people say but I also met my Mr. Wonderful there, so it's not all bad). The profiles that got me to click *like* are the ones with just enough information to make me want to know more. The ones that have no information or worse, just say *hook-up now*, are the ones I don't even bother with. I need to know something— but not everything, if that makes sense.

On the flip side, some guy I don't know who spends the first thirty minutes of a phone conversation talking about himself is definitely not going to be someone I date. Look at your Characters like people your reader is just meeting—no one wants that boring neighbor who drones on and on or the reclusive grump who never says a word. You need to find a good middle ground.

When you have a lot of Backstory, you weigh down your story with long paragraphs of introspection. Have you ever sat at a table and watched someone think? It has to be the most boring thing in the world—like watching paint dry on someone's face. That is exactly what happens with a ton of Backstory. The reader wants things to happen. The reader wants to feel compelled to turn the pages. And most of all, the reader really enjoys uncovering that mystery of what makes the Character tick. Use these tips to avoid dumping a steaming pile of Backstory into the beginning of your novel:

1. **Think of your novel like an onion:** Remember Donkey in *Shrek*? He talks about how donkeys are like parfaits...with layers. Your Characters are like parfaits (or onions) too. They have layers to their personalities, their histories, etc. You want to peel those layers back a little a time, not expose the whole onion (or parfait) in the beginning of the book.

2. **Don't be that crazy neighbor:** Everyone has that one crazy neighbor who tells way more than you want to know about their personal life. The first day you meet them, they're telling you, "My husband ran off with the maid last year. But that's okay because I got him back by slashing his tires. He always said I was too controlling, but hey, I'm an oldest child. I'm used to being in charge. And when I was little, I had to be. My momma was a big-time drug addict, so I had to take care of the little ones. Taught me well, though, because I got pregnant at sixteen and knew just how to raise my own baby. She's flunking out of high school now, but I figure she'll get a job at the McDonald's and be okay until some rich guy comes along and makes her into a wife. That's what I tell her—marry for money, not for love, because when he runs off with the maid, you get half."

- Would you ever go back to her house for coffee again? That kind of immediate openness kinda scares people. And it leaves you with nothing to worry about/wonder about. What if you instead moved in next door, and met the woman, and all she told you was that she admired the way you and your husband talked, and how pretty your house was, but then never invited you into her own, you'd start to wonder. Then you see the neighbor head off to the grocery store, and her husband linger behind, closing the blinds as soon as the maid arrives. Makes you wonder. Then you see the daughter home in the middle of the day when you know she should be at school. Makes you wonder...and suddenly, you're sitting in the chair by the window at the front of the house, watching the neighbor's every day, trying to piece together more of the puzzle.

3. **Every element must work with the Plot:** You've heard me say it before, but I'll say it again—every word in your book, every Scene you choose, every line of Dialogue, every space you describe, *must impact the Plot.* You don't need to talk about Jane Doe's phobia of dogs if there are zero dogs in your story. But if she has to work at an animal shelter, that dog phobia will be important information. Characters' pasts do impact their present, so reveal only the details that impact

them at that moment in the Plot. Don't reveal the dog phobia until she is confronted with animals—and even then, you don't have to tell the whole story behind that or even say she has a phobia. Let the reader wonder why she won't pet that cute little Pekingese.

4. **Characters don't blather about themselves to themselves:** Chances are good that you are either writing your book in first or third person—either way, the reader is in your Characters' heads throughout the story. Think of that as being in your own head. Do you sit there and think, "I should have been the middle child because then Mom would have loved me more and maybe Dad wouldn't have run off with the maid. And I wouldn't be working at this lousy job at McDonald's. I don't even like French fries. How on earth am I going to meet a rich man when I'm working the fryolater? I hope he doesn't have dogs. I'm scared of dogs."

   - When you are in your Character's head, limit their "love-me" thoughts to a minimum. *You* wouldn't sit there and ruminate about yourself and your past, and neither would your Characters. You only think of that time your mother left you in a Sears by accident when you're in Sears and see a child crying. You don't run around thinking about that traumatic event *unless there is a trigger*.

5. **Does this tidbit impact the Character/events at this exact moment?** You don't tell the reader (or hint at)

the Character's childhood fear of dogs when they are about to get on a boat. The dogs have nothing to do with the boat (unless there's a German Shepherd in the captain's chair). Nor do you hint at or tell about the Character's troubled past with her sister when the Character is about to enjoy an intimate moment with a love interest. It's not the time or the place. The Backstory info you choose to add to the book should be triggered by that moment and be an impact on that particular Scene.

- Step back and put yourself in your Character's shoes. Ask yourself, *would I be thinking about X in this particular moment?* If the answer is no, then leave it out. When in doubt, always leave it out. You can add those elements back in later in Revisions if you find they are necessary.

6. **Does this information add Tension to your story?** The key to good Backstory is using it to increase Tension. If your Character is about to walk into a den of wolves, it might be a good time to have them recall the time they were attacked by a wolf hybrid. If the Character is about to kiss their love interest, that's the time to introduce her fear of having her heart broken after her fiancé ran away with the fry cook at McDonald's.

- Along with that, you want to only add enough information to increase Tension. You want to look at how many paragraphs of Backstory you add, because Backstory is, essentially, the Plot's boat just sitting in the water, circling, circling, circling. It's not moving forward; it's not speeding the reader's pulse. It's stagnant.

7. **Are you adding the Backstory at the right place in the action?** Think of a gunfight. When the Characters are shooting it out, *bang, bang, bang,* none of them are going to pause to think about the time they were caught stealing a root beer from the corner shop or the time their mother abandoned them to join the circus. This is a tense, fast-paced moment, and it needs to be treated as such. Later, when things calm down, is the time to add that bit of Backstory. But not too much—as long as there are guns out there, there is inherent Tension, and your Character should be feeling tense and aware, not drifting off into pages and pages of thoughts about the past.

8. **Are you leaving mysteries for the reader?** When a Character hints at a troubled past, the reader is dying to know what happened. Long-running series on television add just a sprinkle of Backstory to each episode, so that you keep coming back to figure out why Jack is so tortured on *Lost* or what Kate is running from.

9. **Is the Backstory in keeping with the Character?** You can't create a Pollyanna whose past includes being locked in a closet most of her life. Think about how the past you have created for your Character would *impact* the person they turn out to be. It has to be believable that they would turn out the way they did, because otherwise no one will believe that your strong kickboxing champion heroine could be taken hostage by the computer nerd at work.

10. **Is the Backstory taking over your page?** Did you write too much? Have too many paragraphs in a row of it? Look at the balance of action and narrative. There's a concept called white space in writing, which in short means how much white space do you see on the page? When a reader looks at pages and pages of dense verbiage, they close the book. It's too much to concentrate on and absorb, especially in today's hurry-up content world. Trim the Backstory and see how much faster and smoother the Scene runs. It's like having too many shrubs in a garden—you miss the cooler parts of the landscaping if it's overrun with greenery. It all becomes one big green blob.

11. **But, but, but…:** I can hear your arguments already. But how will the reader get to know my Character if I don't dump all that information in the beginning? How will they know that she's a nice person? How will they know why he turned into a serial killer?

- Because you *Show instead of Tell* (and we're going to get to how in just a minute). Actions speak a thousand times louder than words, so let your Character *act* instead of *think*. Acting scared around a puppy shows the reader a lot more than the Character standing against the wall thinking endlessly about her dog phobia. Showing a Character snooping around their brother's house instead of having them think about how they don't trust their brother is far more effective. When you Show instead of Tell, you let the reader put the pieces together herself. And that intrigues her to read more, to figure out the entire story.

- Remember this about Backstory: it needs to be *relevant, impactful,* and *believable.* If it fails that three-part test, then take it out. Work it into another place or leave it out altogether. I don't use all the Backstory I create for my Characters, just as no one person in anyone's life knows their entire history, right down to their abject fear of the color taupe. Use the details that matter and let the rest go. The book will be better and stronger for it and the Backstory you do choose to put in will have lots more impact!

Your Turn:

Pick a section of Backstory in your novel and run it through the checklist in this chapter. If it doesn't fit all those parameters, then take it out, or even better, rewrite it so that it moves the Plot forward, shows the Character, and creates a relevant and impactful moment.

Make sure there is a trigger for the memory and an emotional impact on the character.

Scene Analysis

For this scene from *The Homecoming Queen Gets Her Man,* I want you to look at how I layered in Jack's backstory with his childhood, the military, what happened to him, and the heroine. Look at how the memories are active, particularly the memory with Eli. The trigger for that memory is the car door shutting:

> Forgetting. It wasn't something Jack Barlow did easily.
>
> <u>When he was a kid, his grandmother used to tease</u> <u>him about his incredible memory. Looking back,</u> <u>he didn't think that he had such a great memory as</u>

much as a penchant for paying attention to details. That had served him well when he worked in his father's garage and needed to reassemble an engine, and when he'd been on patrol in Afghanistan. In those cases, lives depended upon noticing the smallest things out of place. Still, there were days when he cursed his mind and wished the days would become a blur, the details a blank.

A car door slammed somewhere outside the garage. Jack flinched, oriented his attention in the direction of the sound, adrenaline rushing through his body. To anyone else, it was just a car door, but Jack's brain jogged left instead of right, and in that second, he saw the bright light of the explosion detonating, heard the roaring thunder blasting into the Humvee, then the spray of metal arcing out and away from the impact. Through the floorboards, the passenger seat, up and into—

Eli.

Jack squinted his eyes shut, but it didn't erase the sounds of Eli's agonizing screams, didn't wipe away the sight of his blood on the truck, on Jack, on everything. Didn't make him forget watching Eli's big brown eyes fading from light to glass. Jack shut his eyes, but still all he saw was the moment when he'd turned the truck east instead of west, and the shrapnel intended for Jack hit his best friend instead.

Goddamn.

Jack took in a breath, another, but still his heart jackhammered in his chest, and his lungs constricted. Sweat plastered his shirt, washing him hot, then cold. The wave began to hit him, hard, fast, like a riptide, dragging him under, back to that dark place again.

Blowing out a breath, he unclenched his fists and opened his eyes. He stared up at the underside of the Monte Carlo. The snake lines of the exhaust, the long rectangle of the oil pan. Inhaled the scent of grease, felt the hard cold concrete beneath his palms. Listened to the sounds of passing traffic. Reality.

Finally, Jack pushed himself out from under the car and into the cool, dim expanse of the garage. He rubbed the tired out of his eyes, worked to uncoil the tension that came from snatching a few minutes of sleep every hour. But still the memories stayed, a panther in the shadows.

Ever since he'd come home from the war, Jack had done the only thing he could—worked until he couldn't stay awake. He divided his days between his father's garage and Ray's cottage, because it was only when he was immersed in a disabled engine or surrounded by a stack of unchopped wood that he could pull his mind away.

Away from the past. Away from the mistakes he had made. Away from his own guilt.

And now, away from Meri. He hadn't expected to see her—not today, not ever—and the encounter had left him a little disconcerted, unnerved. Meri represented everything he wanted to put behind him, everything he wanted to forget—

And couldn't.

How the hell was he supposed to tell her the truth? Tell her that he was the one who should have protected Eli, who should have made damned sure Eli, with his perpetual smile, was the one who came home? How could Jack ever look in Meri's eyes and admit the truth?

That it was Jack's fault Eli had died. Jack's, and no one else's.

He threw the wrench in his hands at the workbench. It pinged off the wooden leg and boomeranged into his shin. Jack let out a long string of curses, but it didn't ease one damned bit of the pain.

"Whew. I'm impressed. I usually only hear language like that when the Yankees lose."

Jack turned, grabbing a rag to wipe off the worst of the grease on his hands, and to give him another second to collect himself, push that panther back into the shadows a little more. His brother Luke stood just inside the garage, looking as though he'd just come from the beach, or a vacation, or both. His brown hair had that lightened tint that came from too much time in the sun, and Jack suspected his brother's khaki shorts had more sand in the pockets than dollars. Unlike their eldest brother, Mac, who worked so much, the brothers had nicknamed him Batman, because of how rarely he showed up at family events. "You here to help me change out that transmission?"

Luke laughed. "Work? That's against my religion."

Jack leaned against the tool chest and tossed the rag on a nearby bench. "Funny, I don't remember laziness being a lesson in Sunday school."

"That's because you and Mac were too busy trying to compete for teacher's pet." Luke reached into the small fridge by the door, pulled out two sodas, and tossed one to Jack.

Jack popped the top and took a long swallow of the icy drink. "And you were too busy trying to ditch."

Luke grinned. "Something I have perfected as an adult."

Jack snorted agreement. He swiped the sweat off his brow with the back of his hand and propped a foot against the front bumper of the '87 Monte Carlo. The car had more miles on it than Methuselah had kids, but longtime customer Willie Maddox refused to junk the Great White Whale. The car was big and loud but classic and sporty, and Willie babied his ride like Evangeline Millstone babied her overdressed, overindulged Chihuahua. Hence the new transmission in the Great White Whale, and a decent payday for the garage. Ever since their dad's knee replacement surgery, Jack had been shouldering the garage—and that meant shouldering the responsibility for his father's income. Another week or so and Bobby Barlow would be back in the garage.

"What do you say you knock off early and we head down to Cooter's for a couple beers?"

"It's three o'clock in the afternoon, Luke."

"All the more reason to celebrate." Luke tipped his soda in Jack's direction. "Come on, you workaholic. The world isn't going to fall apart if you close down the shop a couple hours early. Besides, I hear Meri Prescott is back in town. All the more reason to grab a beer with me."

Jack scowled. "What does Meri being back in town have to do with anything?"

"You telling me you aren't interested?" He arched a brow. "Or horny?"

"Jesus, Luke, let it go." Jack tossed the empty soda into the trash, grabbed the wrench and slid back under the Monte Carlo. He tightened a bolt and waited for the sounds of his brother leaving. Instead, a pair of familiar sneakers appeared in his peripheral vision.

"You still gonna stick to the *I'm not interested in her* line?"

"We dated a million years ago." Eight, his mind corrected. "Of course I'm not interested."

Yeah, right. Given the way he'd reacted to seeing her yesterday, and how many times his mind had wandered to thoughts of her, *not interested* was far from the truth. Either way, it didn't matter.

Because getting involved with Meri would mean telling her what had happened to her cousin on that battlefield, and that was one thing Jack couldn't do. Hell, he could barely handle the truth himself. Diving into that deep, dark corner of his mind would pull him down into the abyss, and right now he was barely clinging to the edge.

"Just leave me the hell alone, Luke. I have work to do." There were days when he was glad neither Luke nor Mac had taken to working in the garage. Start talking alternators, and his brothers found other things to do.

It took a while, but eventually Luke's feet moved out of Jack's line of vision, then out of the garage. Quiet descended over the darkened world beneath the Monte Carlo and Jack told himself it brought him peace.

Seems he was just as good at lying as he was at forgetting.

CHAPTER ELEVEN
PLEASE DON'T TELL ME ALL THAT

When I was trying to sell my first book, I amassed quite a collection of rejection letters, most of them saying some variation of the same thing: *the Characters feel flat; they're not three-dimensional; I'm not bonding with the Characters.* I didn't know what any of that meant, or how to fix it. To me, those Characters were alive and well in my head, but I wasn't evoking that same depth on the page for readers. I'd hear feedback about Showing, not Telling, and think to myself, *But I see it in my head when I write it; isn't that Showing?*

No, kids, it's not. Think of it this way—Telling creates a disconnect with the reader. It's dispassionate and flat. Showing, however is all about connection. Showing delivers an emotional bond with the reader, the kind that makes them fall in love with your Characters over and over again.

Telling creates a disconnect with the reader. Showing creates a connection.

You can have the greatest Plot in the world, the best developed Backstory ever for your tortured hero, and still not create a connection with the reader, because you are Telling instead of Showing.

Think of the difference between Showing and Telling this way: You're in Macy's, shopping at the shoe sale, desperately looking for a pair of red wedges, when a perfect stranger comes up and starts telling you her life story. Her daughter is sitting on the floor reading while the mother is monologuing. "I was born in Idaho and moved to Minnesota when I was three. My parents died when I was five, so I went to live with my grandmother..." Are you listening? Probably not. You don't know this woman, and you don't care about her memories of the horse on the farm in Minnesota. You just want to find the shoes and get out of there (and away from this crazy stranger). Oblivious, she keeps droning on and on, telling you her history.

Or...what if the woman comes in with her young daughter and this time, you see they are both clearly disheveled, in clothes that have seen better days, and the little girl is crying. She stumbles over a box and drops her much-loved and much-patched teddy bear beside you. When you turn to give the bear to the little girl, you see a smudge of dirt on her cheeks, the gauntness of her face, and most of all, the sorrow in her eyes. The mother, who looks tired and worn, puts a comforting hand on her daughter's shoulder, and says simply, "I'm so sorry. It's been a long time since someone was kind."

Chances are really good you aren't just going to nod at these two and turn back to the search for red wedges. You're going to sit down with this harried mom and maybe buy her and her daughter some lunch. You're going to listen and ask to hear more. You care because they *Showed* you their history, their inner pain, their worries.

That's the difference between telling and showing. Powerful stuff, isn't it?

It's powerful because telling is passive and doesn't engage or involve the reader. It doesn't make your reader think and care. It slows down your pacing, takes away your action, and also distances your reader from the story.

Showing, however, is active and concrete, creating mental images that bring your story—and your Characters—to life. When you hear about writing that is vivid, evocative, and strong, chances are there's plenty of showing in it. Showing uses all the senses, is interactive, and encourages the reader to participate in the reading experience by drawing her own conclusions.

There are seven signs to look for that will tell you that you are telling:

1. **Those nasty adverbs**: Basically, anything ending in -ly is an adverb. For example:

BEFORE: "You are such a jerk," he said angrily.

First off, you should never modify "said" with an adverb (because that's telling). Second, keep adverb use to a minimum. They're not evil little words that have to be avoided at all costs, but they should be kept to a minimum. Think of them like pepper in a dish. A little is okay; a lot not so much. Either way, it's far better to *show* he was angry:

AFTER: "You are such a jerk." Dan <u>slammed</u> the phone book shut and threw it at the couch. The pages <u>ruffled open</u>, the names inside seeming <u>exposed and vulnerable</u> against the <u>stark black leather</u>. Dan got to his feet, moving so fast his chair <u>skidded</u> against the floor and <u>dented</u> the new drywall.

Do you see the details in the second example? Nowhere did I use the word "angrily" or even "angry." I didn't have to say he was mad. It's pretty clear. In fact, I didn't even have to say he said the words. By showing with his actions right after his dialogue, you know it's him talking.

Now look at the highlighted words. The power in them. The implications of anger in slammed, dented, skidded. There's not even an exclamation point in that, because Dan's actions do all the talking for him. Even if you took the dialogue line out, you'd still know Dan is not a happy person right now.

2. **Using Too Many "To Be" Verbs**: Avoid the forms of this verb—am, is, are, was, was being, will have been, could have been, et al. These not only put you in the passive tense much of the time, but they also tend to remove your reader from the action. Again, they aren't evil words to be avoided at all costs (see I just used the verb myself) but if you can work your writing to make it stronger without the word "was" or any form of it, you'll show more than you tell.

BEFORE: The room was perfect. She saw it and was immediately transported back to her childhood because it had all the elements she remembered.

AFTER: She flung open the wide oak door and stepped into a past from twenty years ago. Linda's breath stilled and everything hushed around her. The bedroom she remembered, down to the last detail. Pink candy-striped walls with white trim. A thick white shag carpet, two plush maroon velvet chairs flanking a silent fireplace. An enormous canopy bed, draped with a sheer white veil. The scent of lilacs hanging in the air. She pressed a hand to her mouth, holding in a gasp. What were the chances? Another room, just like the one she'd had, years ago, before she'd grown up and grown out of the one space that had brought her happiness.

I have a couple of forms of the verb "to be" in there, but the majority of the paragraph doesn't have that at all. You can "see" the room now, though. You can feel it, too, I hope. You can see the details that bring her back to the past, rather than just being told that it does. You can feel her emotional connection. This gives the reader something concrete to visualize and connect with.

3. **Starting with As or -Ing**: Again, as with all of the other examples, this is not a do or die rule either. However, in general, you should avoid starting a sentence with an "As" or "-ing" construction. "As she walked" or "Rapping at the door" are okay beginnings, but *just okay*. They're again, telling, not showing. There's also a little problem those constructions can create with impossible concurrent actions (walking up the hill, he made breakfast—you can't do both at the same time).

BEFORE: Rapping at the door, Elaine made her presence known to the people inside the house.

AFTER: Elaine formed a tight fist with her right hand and pounded on the unforgiving oak. They'd hear her, or she'd break her hand letting them know she'd come to call.

Do you see the tighter imagery in the second example? The stronger beginning? Removing that -ing construction really helps. The same principle applies with "As" constructions.

4. **Just Looking and Feeling**: Looked and felt are great words, but they certainly aren't powerful, and they certainly don't show much. Go back to example one. You could interchange "he looked angry" or "he felt angry" in the "he said angrily" part. Rewriting it without those words is much stronger. Telling the reader someone looks a certain way or feels a certain way is cheating the reader out of drawing her own conclusions. Show the reader and let them interpret.

   Here's a helpful hint: Study movies. In movies, they can't tell you anything. Everything is visual, thus, shown. How do you know someone is upset, angry, happy, sad, frustrated, etc.? Watch movies and write down facial expressions, movements, actions, gestures, etc. Use these to describe your own Characters when you're writing. This is a great way to learn how to show emotion instead of telling it.

5. **Using Anything Other than Said for a Dialogue Tag**: Said is a perfectly good word for a conversation. Why? It becomes invisible. People see it all the time and readers skim over it. When you insert "he exclaimed" or "he screamed" or "he growled," you are telling the reader how the Character is acting instead of showing.

Yes, you can use them from time to time (meaning, *very* rarely) but not all the time. It's a very quick mark of a newbie writer.

Instead, you have two choices: Use "he said" or "she said" or use an action tag. Following is an example that uses both to rewrite a passage:

BEFORE: "You're a jerk," Joe grumbled. "You never tell me anything."

"I do, too," Jeremy whined.

"Yeah? Then how come I didn't know there was a party tonight? How come I wasn't invited?" Joe shouted. He started to cry and dropped into a chair.

"It's okay," Jeremy soothed. "It's okay. You can still give me a gift."

Granted, that's an extreme example, but honest to goodness, I have read passages just like that in contests I have judged. Let's try this again, without the telling dialogue tags.

AFTER: Joe flung the empty beer can across the room. It pinged off the armchair and dropped onto the tile floor with a clatter, then rolled under the table with the four others that had also missed the trash can. "Jeremy, you're a jerk. You never tell me anything." He reached for another beer, <u>popped</u> the top. Didn't bother to give one to Jeremy.

"I do, too." Jeremy <u>plopped</u> onto the couch, <u>flipped</u> on the TV and started <u>sofa surfing</u>.

"Oh, yeah?" Joe <u>ripped</u> the remote out of Jeremy's hands. "Then how come I didn't know there was a party tonight for your birthday? How come I wasn't even invited? What kind of friend does that crap?" He <u>tossed</u> the remote into an empty chair and <u>spun</u> away.

Jeremy didn't say anything for a long time. <u>A skinny guy on *Jerry Springer* ranted in the background</u>. "I'm sorry," he said. "But look at the bright side."

Joe <u>spun</u> back and <u>hated himself for letting hope rise in his chest</u>. For still caring what Jeremy had to say. "What bright side?"

Jeremy stood up and grinned, that <u>cocky one-sided smile that begged forgiveness and said he knew he had the upper hand in the relationship, all at the same time</u>. "You can still buy me a gift. And I'll bring you some leftover cake."

Then he headed out the door. But not before Joe <u>pitched</u> his <u>half-full</u> beer can at Jeremy's head. And this time, had <u>damned good</u> aim.

Look at the power words that are used in that passage. You know a lot about Jeremy from the details that I used, and the way he acts. There's some telling in that, when you are in Joe's Point of View and he hates himself for having hope, but by and large, the actions and dialogue *show* the reader their relationship. I only had to use said once, and instead chose to use action tags to anchor the dialogue.

6. **Creating Passive Characters**

Showing is about *action*. In the before/after above, the Characters actions show their emotions. What does Jeremy's plopping onto the couch and flipping channels show? Do we know he doesn't care, without telling the reader? Yes, we do, because his actions show his emotions.

7. **Creating Inactive Introspection**

Even in introspection, you should have showing instead of telling. It's all about painting a picture in the reader's mind, not just of the Scene but the *impact* of that Scene on the Character. Here's a snippet from my book, *When Somebody Loves You*. There's action, even in a Scene that starts out mostly in the hero's head, and the impact on him is shown in the words I chose:

Learning to show instead of tell takes practice, but eventually it becomes more intuitive. When you feel like the Scene is flat, or that you aren't connecting with your Characters, go back over this list of seven and see if any apply to the troublesome passage.

Your Turn:

Take a simple phrase like "It was hot." Rewrite it without the word *was*. Better yet, don't even use the word *hot*. Think of all the things you can use to describe heat, the scents, sounds, sights that are associated with heat. Make a list, if you want. Then write a few sentences that show the weather was hot.

Scene Analysis

Hunter McCoy stood on the front porch of the small white farmhouse that sat at the edge of the Silver Spur, sipping a cup of coffee and watching the sun rise. He'd watched near every sunrise behind his property, for as long as he could remember. Course, when he was a boy, he'd watched the sunrise with a mug of chocolate milk, standing tall and straight next to his dad and his granddad, pretending he was holding a cup of coffee like the men he'd so admired. Now it was just him running the Silver Spur. But that hadn't stopped the morning tradition. In Hunter's mind, it was a way to commune with his father and grandfather, maybe soak in a little of their wisdom as the sun crested over the trees at the far side of the land that had been in the McCoy family for as many generations as the state of Georgia had been in the union.

The sun started like a shy child, peeking between the trees, washing a slight gold over the long squat stables, the smooth oval training corral, the old red barn, the blooming flowers in the far pasture, then finally reaching tentative fingers across the lawn, up to the steps of the porch. The birds chattered in the trees, rising in volume as the land went from dim to bright. The horses nickered in their stalls, and from far down the road, Joey Barrett's rooster crowed. At Hunter's feet, Foster, a furry lump of a dog that was part golden retriever, part moocher, snoozed in the early morning light.

CHAPTER TWELVE
MAKE EVERY DETAIL MATTER

We've covered a lot of the basics so far—Characters, Goal, Motivation, Conflict, Scenes, Backstory. Among all of those, however, is the power of detail. Using a specific detail instead of a general one can greatly impact your book.

Details in the Setting

When done right, Setting is a Character tool, not just window dressing. Think about that—it's not decoration. It's a Plot tool, used to further your Characters and show not tell.

> Setting should be used to show the impact of that place on the Character and how he/she is changed/affected/not affected.

It's about more than just putting a claustrophobic Character into a tight space. It's about using everything from the backyard where the heroine used to play as a child to the police car where the hero was arrested after a crazy summer night when he was a kid, and using this to show how the Character is impacted. Does this place make him nervous? Strong? Excited?

And after the Characters experience these feelings, what do they do? Do they run? Confront their fears? Become more afraid and thus, retreat into a deeper shell?

Now, telling you to have your Setting affect your Character and then having you walk away from this chapter and actually *employing* that technique are two different things. To learn how to do that, try writing a Scene that has nothing to do with your current work, putting your Character into a new Setting—a scary place or a new place or something where the Character has to use skills he or she has never used before. This will allow you to play with this technique and then go back and use it with your other work.

When you are working with Setting, here are some other tips to keep in mind:

1. **Weave in your narrative throughout your descriptions.** It's boring to just read a travelogue of what the place looks like. Work in some history—your Characters weren't born in a vacuum. Let the hero see the tree he climbed as a kid, the neighbor's house that is a different color every spring, the blank lot that used

to hold a favorite haunt. Each of these memories will show a bit more about your Character.

2. **Add in actions, too, throughout descriptions.** Don't have your Characters stand in one place and just look around. Let them move, interact with the Setting. Then you pepper the Scene with the Setting details, rather than blanketing the reader with adjectives and hoping they can find the action among the descriptions.

3. **Use all your senses—and know how your Character uses their senses.** When a bloodhound enters a room, the first thing he uses is his nose to scope out the place. Think about your Characters—what do they notice first? The touch? Smell? Colors?

4. **Have a Character revisit a Setting later in the book.** By then, your Character will have changed and grown and will see that place differently. Show that new impact on him/her.

5. If your Setting descriptions aren't working right, **try having a different Character's viewpoint to see them.** Sometimes, the Character you are using for the Scene isn't the right one. Try changing viewpoints and see what you get.

6. **Use visual cues.** I save catalogs and bookmark websites so I can remember what an apartment filled with Crate & Barrel or Pier I Imports purchases might look like. I like to immerse myself with that visual before writing

the Scene. I'll also use scent cues (lighting a candle, brewing some coffee) if I want to describe a detail accurately.

7. If you're describing a familiar place, **be sure you're not skimping on details.** Sometimes, we know a place so well that we forget to describe the sounds of traffic passing by or the quiet of the street in the mid-afternoon. Try to go back and re-read with a stranger's eyes or have someone who doesn't live in that area read the passage and give you feedback.

8. **If you're describing a place where you have never been, do your research.** Talk to people who live there, read books, study maps. Don't rely entirely on the Internet. Look at the newspapers, magazines, etc. for the area to see what's going on now in that area. Do a search for web cams in the area to see if there's a live visual of the streets.

9. **Layer your Settings with nuances and details.** The best way to evoke a powerful Setting is to put in some punch with small details (not overloading with tons of description). Naming the plants instead of just saying "shrubs" or mentioning the cobblestones on the sidewalk, etc., all help your reader get more of a sense of the place.

10. **Read people who do Setting well**: Amy Tan, Eudora Welty, Pat Conroy, John Updike, Sinclair Lewis. Learn

from those who have gone before you and try to incorporate their great lessons into your own work.

One important point: *only spend time describing the Setting if that spot impacts the Plot.* That means you don't waste gobs of time describing the gardens when the murder takes place in the museum down the street. You can do a line or two about the gardens, to give a feel to the location as your Character's walking through them, but don't spend paragraphs on a place that has nothing to do with the Plot. You waste the reader's time, your time, and you clutter up your book with unnecessary details.

Using Details in the Narrative

As I mentioned earlier, Showing builds that emotional connection with your reader because it makes them care, and when they care, they keep reading. They root for your Character. They cry when the book ends. And most of all, they buy your next book and tell all their friends to do the same. When readers care, they bond with your Characters. That bond is an unquantifiable, impossible-to-force, and a vital part of compelling books. Details—strategically placed and impactful—are the biggest key to strong Showing.

One of the big problems I see writers making is what details they choose to focus on. They either choose just one type of detail, like describing every single room the Character walks into, or they put in so few that it's hard for the reader to become invested in the Scene. Here are five key points about using details in your Scenes:

Details Must Have a Purpose: I've mentioned before that I feel strongly that every single word in your book should be worth the reader's time. They are reading your book instead of talking to their kids or hanging out with friends or being with their spouse. They are giving you the gift of hours of their life, which is an extraordinarily precious gift. So don't waste it, and make every detail matter.

> How do you do that? Simple. Adhere to one key rule: the details you choose should all be about *emotional impact* on the Character. We are affected by the things we see, smell, touch. We don't go blithely about our business, never being reminded of that old lover or that tragic day. The things/people we encounter are reminders, either of where we've been, where we are, or where we are going. For example, the scent of fresh-baked homemade bread always reminds me of my late mother and the easy conversations we would have in the kitchen while she kneaded and shaped the dough. My mother passed away a long time ago and our relationship was complicated, so that scent and sight of fresh bread is bittersweet and impactful.

If you haven't read *Mystic River* by Dennis Lehane, you should. He is an impactful author because he uses details in a powerful way. In *Mystic River*[7], there are three friends growing up in Boston. Sean becomes a cop, Dave becomes a little lost, and Jimmy becomes a mobster. There's a Backstory Scene with the three boys playing catch by the subway. Not only is Lehane's Backstory powerful because it's vivid and active, not a bunch of narrative, but it also foreshadows who these people will become. A little backstory: Jimmy is a risk-taker, a guy who has no fear, and in this Scene where the boys lose the ball on the subway tracks, a Scene told through Sean's Point of View, his Character is already vivid and strong:

> Sean heard a thick rumble that could have been a train entering the tunnel up at Washington Street or could have been trucks rolling along the street above, and the people on the platform heard it too. They waved their arms, whipped their heads around to look for the subway police. One guy placed a forearm across his daughter's eyes.
>
> Jimmy kept his head down, peering into the darkness under the platform for the ball. He found it. He wiped some black grime off it with his shirtsleeve and ignored the people kneeling on the yellow line, extending their hands down toward the track.

---

7   Dennis Lehane, *Mystic River* (Duluth, William Morrow, 2003), 416.

Dave nudged Sean and said, "Whew, huh?" too loud.

Jimmy walked along the center of the track toward the stairs at the far end of the platform, where the tunnel opened gaping and dark, and a heavier rumble shook the station, and people were jumping now, banging fists into their hips. Jimmy took his time, strolling really, then he looked back over his shoulder, caught Sean's eyes, and grinned.

What do we know about Jimmy from this snippet? He's fearless. He's cavalier. He doesn't care what people think, yet he knows what they are thinking about him (hence the grin). He's going to take the risks and do the things that no one else will do. Later in the Plot, this is a huge factor, so Lehane is laying fabulous groundwork here.

Your details are there to help you achieve something on the page, whether it's to show a Character's emotional growth, or the fear that is holding them back. What the Character sees and focuses on in a Scene is used to demonstrate something important about the Character, something the reader should know or be able to infer from the Scene. Jimmy doesn't focus on the people's reactions—he focuses on doing what it takes to continue the game with his friends. They are his family, essentially, and he risks everything for that, but with a confidence that says he knows it will be fine in the end. His Character is so strongly delineated from the others on that page, that you can connect and relate to him, and most of all, care about him, because there's a pretty intense Plot about to happen. It also nicely foreshadows what happens later in the book, without being an obvious foreshadow.

Details Should Make the Moment Real: A great writer will show smoke, show heat, show burning timbers, and the reader will feel the fear of a fire closing in on them. The description will invoke the fire, rather than the author saying "there was a fire," which is Telling. Even better, don't just focus on the details of the fire, but the impact on the Characters. What are they feeling? Are they trying to scramble away? Huddle in a corner? Screaming for help? Their actions, augmented by details (a hoarse throat, screams being swallowed by the flames) can create a far more powerful Scene than saying "she was scared." However, what makes it real is…you guessed it… emotional impact.

One teeny line in Joshilyn Jackson's *The Almost Sisters*[8], where the main Character has found out she's pregnant, easily sums up the feelings she has about being a thirty-eight-year-old unwed mother in a family of overachievers:

- I sat staring at a wall covered with smiling rabbits and baby deer in cotton candy colors.

---

8   Joshilyn Jackson, *The Almost Sisters* (New York, HarperCollins, 2017), 352.

The raccoons all looked so smug, like they were laughing at me.

The Character is sitting in a pediatrician's waiting room, and you can see the pastels and the happy forest Scene in the wallpaper, but for Leia, they are all an example of the condemnation she feels for herself and is dreading from her family. You can have that same emotional impact and connection and show that this moment is super real for the Character, with a single line. This happens in the moment in the waiting room when she finally accepts that she's pregnant and realizes that it's going to mess up her life.

Details Should Focus on an Important Memory: Ask anyone the moment they knew they were in love with their spouse, or the day they met their best friend, chances are good they can recall that specific moment, from the weather to what they were wearing, to the music on the radio. Our brains file special moments away with all kinds of details and resurrects them every time that memory comes up—like when you go to a wedding and think of your own wedding day.

- This works for good and bad memories for your Characters. Maybe a shadowed alley reminds your heroine of the day she was attacked, or maybe the snide comment by a co-worker reminds your hero of being bullied in middle school. Those details from that moment helps ground the memory and add the emotion it needs.

In my book *The Sweetheart Bargain,* one of my secondary Characters celebrates a birthday, which triggers a memory of her late father.

> Greta Winslow celebrated her eighty-third birthday the way she celebrated most everything: with a heaping plate of windmill cookies and a double shot of Maker's Mark. Her father had been a Jim Beam man. He'd line up his empty liters along the top of the kitchen cabinets, and as the collection grew, they created a prism when the morning light first hit. When Greta was a little girl, she'd sit at the scarred kitchen table, the one with the black divot in the center from one of Uncle Abe's forgotten cigarettes, and watch the dance of colors. By the time her father died at the ripe old age of ninety-seven, the bottle row was two, some places three deep, but the rainbow still came every morning. Greta missed that rainbow. Missed her daddy something fierce, too. So she started her day the way her father always had. With a few nips of the hard stuff.

Details Should Matter to that Particular Character: When you choose what your Character is going to focus on in a Scene, it must be things that matter to them in some way, shape, or form. All of the details will filter through that Character's past and present. For instance, a Character who has been orphaned at a young age will see a family in a park differently than a harried mom with three toddlers. A claustrophobic will see a closet very differently from a Character who doesn't have a fear of small spaces. A man who has a fear of heights (e.g. Richard Gere in Pretty Woman) will view a fire escape on an apartment building a lot differently than a fireman who runs up and down them all the time. A Character who hasn't been outside much will feel differently about a sunny day than one who has a hangover and isn't up to the sun being in his face. The Characters' descriptions of these places will be different too because they will be imbued with their thoughts, feelings, and emotions about the place.

Whatever you choose to describe, make sure it's something that matters to that Character—and matters to the Plot. This small snippet from David Joy's *The Weight of This World*[9] shows the Character's focus on money and his impoverished state:

- If he'd had any money, he would've bought Thad something too. Of course, if he'd had more money, he would've bought a second biscuit himself. But aside from a few hundred dollars stashed away that he wouldn't touch, all Aiden had was ninety-four cents to his name. He'd counted it while the acne-faced kid wrapped his order up and pushed the bag across

---

9   David Joy, *The Weight of This World* (New York, Penguin Publishers, 2017), 272.

the counter. That first sausage biscuit cost $1.22 after taxes, so Aiden just asked for a few extra packs of grape jelly, shook his head, and cussed his way through the door when the teenager told him that would cost him another fifty cents.

Details Should Add, not Detract: Before you decide to describe that chair in the corner, ask yourself why you are describing it. Does it intensify the mood? Draw the Character more fully? Make an action more powerful? Advance the Plot? Expose the Character's inner fears? If it doesn't, then consider cutting those words and instead writing ones that do what you need your words to do.

White Oleander[10] by Janet Fitch is chock-full of beautiful language—all of which works hard on the page. The powerful words she chooses are a nice echo to the main Character's complicated relationship with her mother. The Santa Ana winds are a metaphor for the crazy, unpredictable life she has.

> The Santa Anas blew in hot from the desert, shriveling the last of the spring grass into whiskers of pale straw. Only the oleanders thrived, their delicate poisonous blooms, their dagger green leaves. We could not sleep in the hot dry nights, my mother and I, and I woke up at midnight to

---

10   Janet Fitch, *White Oleander* (New York, Little, Brown & Co., 1999), 446.

find her bed empty. I climbed to the roof and easily spotted her blond hair like a white flame in the light of the three-quarter moon.

Good showing instead of telling is always about the details, but choosing which details to include and which to omit is the key to powerful showing. I am constantly trying to find better ways to describe and more powerful uses for the words I choose. If I read a book that has really good descriptive phrases in it, I often buy a second copy so I can mark it up with my highlighter. Not so I can memorize and copy the author's work later, but so I can analyze his/her technique and try to apply those lessons to my own work. For instance, in *White Oleander*, there's one Scene where a poinsettia is compared to the blood spatter from a gunshot. That's a unique description that stayed with me long after I put down the novel. I made a note to myself to try to find more unique ways of describing things — to go beyond the typical crimson river of blood and find something more evocative.

Powerful showing draws the reader into the story and engages her on a deeper level. Be sure the details are important, and are ones that make the book/Scene more powerful, and your writing will have that powerful impact you wanted!

Your Turn:

Pick a pivotal moment in your book. How can you use the details that your main Character is noticing to increase the emotional impact? Try narrowing down to a few specific items, and then show how that impacts them.

BONUS CHAPTER
REVISING SMARTER

I've dumped most of my writing knowledge into the pages of this book, but there's one more thing I want to talk about. Revision. Once you've written your book, the next thing you must do is *revise* it. The real writing comes in Revision, not in the first draft, contrary to what people might think, or at least it does for me. I know that it can be tempting to just get the book off your desk already, but take a step back and think about why revising can be the best thing you ever do for your writing.

Revision teaches you an incredible amount. It teaches you how to edit, how to fix, how to tear apart and mend. Kind of like when you learn to knit, and your hat starts looking more like a sock, so you have to undo seventeen rows of stitches and start again. In order to fix your hat, you need to go back and figure out where you messed up, retrace your steps, analyze your mistakes, then fix them. Chances are good you won't keep making the same mistakes, or if you do, you'll correct them sooner.

Revision also makes you a stronger writer, sort of like going to the gym. The first time you work out, you lift the five-pound weights. Second time, you lift the eight-pound weights. After a month of working out regularly, you're working your way up to arm curls with the thirty-pound dumbbells and those five-pounders are collecting dust. Revision works the same. The more you do it, the stronger your writing becomes.

I'm not going to tell you that Revision itself is easy. It's not. But when you go to write the next book, and the one after that, having revised the one before, you will have learned a lot and more of the writing process will happen in your head. I've published more than eighty books, but I've written more than ninety. The process becomes more intuitive the more you learn your weaknesses and how to course correct.

Okay, so how and when should you go about revising? Opinions on this are as divided as the transcontinental highway system. I'll tell you what works for me, and you can do what you want from there.

I mean that literally by the way—every author should do what works for them. Don't copy my method, get frustrated, and give up. Remember, this is your book, and sometimes each book, and each type of writing requires a different approach. Be flexible. Be yourself.

> Tailor your writing process to what works for your lifestyle, your way of thinking, your time crunches.

I do a total of three passes on my books, for three different stages and reasons.

Revision #1:

I revise—a little—as I write, meaning that I'll edit a word that doesn't sound right, delete a Scene that simply isn't flowing, start over again from another Character's Point of View if the first one doesn't work. But I don't do any major, Plot-changing Revisions until I am at about a third of the way through the book.

Do I measure this? No. I've learned instinctually where that point is. I feel it in my gut. I could be eighty pages into a 200-page book, or fifty pages. This point is where the honeymoon period has worn off and my Characters, who seemed so dreamy and amazing when I began writing, are starting to become irritating and stubborn.

How do I know I'm at this point?

Because I'm stalled. I can't progress forward. The Characters won't move. Won't talk. There's a stalemate in the Plot and I'm not quite sure where to turn next. That's how I know it's time to go back and revise, because by doing so I'll unearth all the clues I need to press forward.

I print out the book and read it on paper, because I see things differently and hear the cadence of the words differently when it's printed than when it's on my computer screen. I make scribbles in the margins and mark the things I want to come back to later. This is when I start planning my Characters and truly getting to know them. What makes them tick? What are they afraid of? What is their Worst Nightmare? If I haven't already figured out the external and Internal Goal, Motivation, and Conflict, I work on that.

Yes, I will toy with this word, tweak that paragraph, but in the beginning, I am still building the book, and so I only look for the big stuff.

Revision #2:

My second major Revision is done at the two-thirds point of the book. Again, I know this point instinctually because I get stuck again, and I'm finding any possible reason not to write. I start cleaning closets and drawers or organizing my spices. I fiddle with the same page over and over again, unable to move forward.

So I go back and print it again, going through all the same steps as I just did in the first Revision, and as I do, I start finding some nuggets of information. This is usually the point where I surprise myself by finding all these cool little things that my subconscious layered throughout the manuscript. I make little notes again and keep track of the elements that I want to work into the last third of the book. For instance, is my heroine avoiding the garden because it reminds her of the day her mother died? Well, I'm definitely going to give her something that puts her in that garden again. I'm also looking for sets of three—if I mention something like a memory or a Character, I want to use it three times (there's a psychological reason why readers remember things in threes). If it's an important emotional element, I make a note to use it at the end of the book.

If you're having trouble finding these nuggets of Character reveals, look deep. Do you have a Character who refuses to talk about a certain issue in his past, yet is continually drawn to the same room in the house?

Bingo. There's a subconscious clue. Whatever that issue is has something to do with that room. That's why your subconscious laid the tracks—so your mental train could travel them. Look around for a few more clues and then write a confrontation Scene between that Character and another, in that very room.

I bet you'll find your issue.

If you don't, try giving the Character a prop. A photograph. A box of mementos. A letter. These are the things that will trigger the train to start moving, because as your Character discovers the truth underneath it all so too will you as the author. It's often a great Plot twist, too. I have used the prop thing many times to force myself and my Characters to uncover the real fears they aren't facing. I discover it just as they do, which is kind of fun.

This two-thirds point Revision is, to me, my most important Revision. It's the one where I start truly figuring out the Plot and everything that's going awry. It's where I begin digging deep into who my Characters are, and making sure that I have a Goal in every Scene, and rising stakes at the end of those Scenes.

If you are stuck at this same point, chances are very good that it's a Plot problem. Start by analyzing your overall book-length Goal, Motivation, and Conflict, then going into each Scene and making sure it has a Goal that feeds into the book-length Goal. Go back to what you learned about Scene and Sequel and ask yourself if things are getting worse on all levels—Externally, Internally, and romantically or suspense-wise, depending on your genre.

Remember, the Character's weaknesses cause their problems over and over again. A Character who says yes when she wants to say no will get herself into trouble time and time again. A hero who is a loose cannon will do things that alienate others or take risks that jeopardize his life. These weaknesses are part of what helps you escalate the Tension, so use them to your advantage.

At the two-thirds point in the book, the Characters' Strengths are starting to appear. These are what will save the day in the last third of the book, so make a note of them, and the lessons you want your Characters to learn through all those mistakes they keep making.

The Final Revision:

My last Revision takes place just before the final Scene in my book. I can't write the very last Scene until I have completely revised all the pages before. I know, it sounds odd, but I never write that last one until I've gone back through the entire book one more time.

Why? Because I don't know how the story ends until I have tidied up all that came before, and unearthed all the other clues. I complete the same steps as before, this time going deeper than ever before, really looking to flesh out my Characters.

One of the main questions I ask myself at this point is:

Have I gotten the maximum emotional bang for my buck out of this Scene?

It doesn't matter what emotion you're talking about, whether it's humor, sadness, or anger. I want to wring as much out of the big Scenes as I can, so I go back and power up the language, the Character details, the Showing, the Pacing, etc. to be sure that Scene is at its best.

Then, when all the changes are inputted and the Revisions are done, I read the last couple chapters over one more time, because that gets my mental train roaring to the finish, and then I write the very last Scene.

I try to echo something I've written in the beginning (most of the time, not always) or bring back some emotional tie to another big Scene in the book, before I wrap everything up. Then I read that over, do any other tweaks, sit back, listen to my gut (which usually says "I'm hungry" at this point) and if my gut says it's done, I call the book done and send it off to my editor.

And as soon as possible, start the next one, hopefully as a wiser, more experienced author!

ABOUT THE AUTHOR

Shirley Jump is an award-winning, *New York Times, Wall Street Journal,* Amazon, and *USA Today* bestselling author who has published more than 70 books in 24 countries. Her most recent books hit #1 in two categories on Amazon, and her Christmas novella hit the *USA Today* list in November. Her books have received multiple awards and kudos from authors such as Jayne Ann Krentz, who called her books "real romance," Virginia Kantra, who said, "Shirley Jump packs lots of sweet and plenty of heat in this heartwarming first book of her promising new series," and Jill Shalvis, who called *The Sweetheart Bargain* "a fun, heartwarming small town romance that you'll fall in love with."

As the owner of JumpStart Creative Solutions, Shirley also does book building, content editing, ghostwriting, and author coaching. She has spoken all over the world about the power of narrative and how to create compelling books. A former reporter, she has a background in all aspects of writing, from hard news to publicity to fiction. Visit her website at www. ShirleyJump.com or see her on Facebook, Twitter, Instagram and LinkedIn @ShirleyJump.

DOWNLOAD MY FREE HANDOUT

"The Highlighter Method of Learning to Plot" at JumpStartCreativeSolutions.com

Lightning Source UK Ltd.
Milton Keynes UK
UKHW010700030422
401004UK00001B/273